formatio

TRADITION. EXPERIENCE.
TRANSFORMATION.

Formatio books from InterVarsity Press follow the rich tradition of the church in the journey of spiritual formation. These books are not merely about being informed, but about being transformed by Christ and conformed to his image. Formatio stands in InterVarsity Press's evangelical publishing tradition by integrating God's Word with spiritual practice and by prompting readers to move from inward change to outward witness. InterVarsity Press uses the chambered nautilus for Formatio, a symbol of spiritual formation because of its continual spiral journey outward as it moves from its center. We believe that each of us is made with a deep desire to be in God's presence. Formatio books help us to fulfill our deepest desires and to become our true selves in light of God's grace.

JOYFUL EXILES

LIFE IN CHRIST ON THE DANGEROUS EDGE OF THINGS

JAMES M. HOUSTON

IVP Books

An imprint of InterVarsity Press
Downers Grove, Illinois

InterVarsity Press
P.O. Box 1400, Downers Grove, IL 60515-1426
World Wide Web: www.ivpress.com
E-mail: email@ivpress.com

InterVarsity Press® *is the book-publishing division of InterVarsity Christian Fellowship/USA*®*, a student movement active on campus at hundreds of universities, colleges and schools of nursing in the United States of America, and a member movement of the International Fellowship of Evangelical Students. For information about local and regional activities, write Public Relations Dept., InterVarsity Christian Fellowship/USA, 6400 Schroeder Rd., P.O. Box 7895, Madison, WI 53707-7895, or visit the IVCF website at <www.intervarsity.org>.*

All Scripture quotations, unless otherwise indicated, are taken from the Holy Bible, New International Version®. NIV®. *Copyright* ©*1973, 1978, 1984 by International Bible Society. Used by permission of Zondervan Publishing House. All rights reserved.*

Design: Cindy Kiple
Images: Pete Turner/Getty Images

ISBN-10: 0-8308-3324-2
ISBN-13: 978-0-8308-3324-5

Printed in the United States of America ∞

Library of Congress Cataloging-in-Publication Data

Houston, J. M. (James Macintosh), 1922-
 Joyful exiles: life in Christ on the dangerous edge of things /
James M. Houston.
  p. cm.
 Includes bibliographical references and index.
 ISBN-13: 978-0-8308-3324-5 (cloth: alk. paper)
 1. Christian life. I. Title.
 BV4501.3.H683 2006
 248.4—dc22
                                                                    2006020860

P	19	18	17	16	15	14	13	12	11	10	9	8	7	6	5	4	3	2	1
Y	21	20	19	18	17	16	15	14	13	12	11	10	09	08	07	06				

To Chris and Jean,
who share prayerfully
as joyous exiles

Contents

Preface

Western secularism's radical inclusiveness is sweeping over us, causing Western Christianity to drift farther away from biblical faith than it has ever been. This drift, which presents one of the greatest challenges facing the Christian church, is occurring not only outside us, but within our own spirits. So it is no surprise that Christians today are terribly confused, both as individuals and institutions. Some people see this clearly. Others are in denial, making the situation worse by heading precipitously in the wrong direction, even though their intentions may be good. In the confusion, those that would speak prophetically are judged presumptuous, while pragmatic voices are considered realistic. The purpose of the following essays is not only to shout out in alarm but also, on a more modest level, to bear witness to what I have tried to live out in the past eight decades as I've sought to follow Christ. If this personal narrative articulates and confirms any heartfelt issues that you also sense, it will serve its purpose.

I have written these essays in the genre of dialogue so that you can readily engage with the ideas presented. In the appendix you will find ways to further explore the role of dialectics in personal communication about faith. All the royalties from all my books, including this one, are donated to the Institute of Religion and Culture, which has been established to provide educational grants for young Christians in key situations who illustrate the principles I am describing in this book. If you desire to communicate with me, please visit the website we have established for this purpose at <www.religionandculture.org>.

We live not only personally but publicly. The public aspect of Christian life should foster our growth in Christ, but instead it seems to create confusion. "I go to church, but . . . " "I serve this organization, but . . . " "I train at this theological college, but . . . " "I believe in Christian ministry, but . . . " Why do we qualify our expressions of faith? Why indeed do we question the institutional structures throughout our society? This book is for the "exiles," those who need the moral courage to move away from the familiar and the conventional and into the dangerously exposed places, to prophetically critique our cultural norms and institutional attitudes.

Faithfulness to biblical convictions always calls us to live "dangerously on the edge" of our culture. This is not a call to individualism and independence of spirit. It is an invitation to experience more deeply what it means to become a faithful witness to Christ. This process requires that we have the moral courage and selflessness to confront cultural challenges, resisting the insidious pressure to depend on techniques instead of the love and Spirit of God. It requires that we foster spiritual friendship and allow community to grow spiritually rather than be organized artificially. It demands that we be more personally available to others in sharing the joy of God's salvation.

Some twenty years ago I asked Malcolm Muggeridge, then near the end of his life, if he regretted anything about his life as an author. He replied that he wished he had written "against consensus"—as if he had not been the great lampoonist of society as editor of *Punch*.

"I mean," he continued, "against conventional religious consensus." He had been a late convert to Christ and left this task undone. "But you should do it," he added. I laughed incredulously at this inconceivable assignment.

Perhaps Malcolm sowed a mustard seed that is now grown into a small plant. This book is the confessions of a life spent recklessly, and it is intended to support and encourage other joyous exiles who may feel as I did in response to Muggeridge: as if they were being exhorted to engage in mission impossible. It is my hope that these joyous exiles, though they may be hidden in small groups in diverse settings, continue to grow into a global network of friendships.

It is to such that I myself am indebted in writing this book. Invidious as it is to select names, I am particularly grateful for the editorial support of Bob Fryling, publisher of InterVarsity Press, of Gary Deddo, who has been my skillful editor, and of his team. Helpful reviews of my manuscript have been provided by Pat Calvo, Darrell Johnson, Dean Overman, Bill Reimer, Skip Ryan, Paul Helm and, lastly, Sally Voorhies.

I am thankful for my own family and for loyal friends who continue to give encouragement. Kelly Barbey, Craig Gay, Chris Houston, Keith Martin and Ken Stevenson serve on the board of the Institute of Religion and Culture, established to promote the explorations here presented. But whatever errors of interpretation and fact remain in this book are solely the responsibility of the author.

Prologue

Why Dialectics?

Our interest's on the dangerous edge of things.

ROBERT BROWNING,
Bishop Blougram's Apology

*Moses replied, . . . "I wish that all the LORD's people were prophets
and that the LORD would put his Spirit on them!"*

NUMBERS 11:29

A while back my son asked me to write out the basic convictions I
have sought to live out in my Christian faith. This book is the response
to his request. It outlines the inner dialogue I have exercised over many
years, expressed in six essays that are arranged dialectically in three
parts: "Responding to the Christian Faith" (which is hidden and yet
open), "Challenging our Culture" (which is publicly surreal and so must
become personally real) and "Maintaining the Christian Faith" (both in
communal expression and personal transmission). Each essay in turn
contains its own inner dialectics. For example, faith is hidden yet not
underground, personal yet not individualistic and so on.

WHY THE GENRE OF DIALOGUE?

Our postmodern society is in a state of reaction against monologue, neg-

atively associating it with ideology. The parade of "isms" has flattened all
the perspectives and attitudes of the human condition into one social absolute, variously described in the past century as socialism, Marxism and
fascism, and now manifested as fundamentalism, liberalism and even
secularism. The rise of the individual, together with the shift from an
elite culture to a mass culture, indeed a "pop" culture, encourages everyone to have a voice so that we can all argue and respond to everyone else.
A family today no longer practices the adage that "children should be
seen but not heard."

Even the author of a book is no longer a sole communicator. What
you as a reader get from a book may not be what the author intended to
communicate, because your reading is filtered through all your own experiences and relationships. This has always been true, but today the individualism of the reader is more articulated than before. We all put up
defenses against reality, blocking what we don't want to take in and se-
lecting what we do want to hear, read or know.

Dialogue, then, is a way we can express our own perceptions and values. We do this both with other people and individually in soliloquy
with ourselves. Indeed, as social beings we cannot be personal without
living together in dialogue. This is certainly the married way of life. Rita,
my wife, is always refusing to accept things at face value—especially my
unsupported opinion! Dialogue is just this: engaging in discussion to
promote and deepen the personal dimension of living together, even
when our viewpoints are not the same.

The dialectic genre enables us to see truth in multifaceted ways. Like
Job, we must often refuse to accept the foolish platitudes of the worldly-
wise who presume to express the ways of God. The preaching from our
pulpits commonly continues to be made up of clichés and generalizations, and the radical changes taking place in our culture make it more
difficult for teachers and pastors to communicate unilaterally from a po-

sition of authority. So I find it essential to use dialectics as an exchange between my own experiences and others', to test their validity. (See the appendix for further reading on dialectics.)

INVERSE DIALECTICS OF THE CHRISTIAN LIFE

Increasingly, then, true Christian faith must be countercultural. We may have to forfeit our careers, some of our friends, even our freedom if we are to remain true to the Christian convictions placed within us by God's Spirit. Through the Christian (inverse dialectic) we are constantly reminded of our status as strangers and pilgrims in this world who seek one to come. It is in antithesis to the world that we are in resonance with heaven. That is why we are joyful exiles; we have another, better home, a more glorious destiny.

What most of us lack is not knowledge of the faith but the spiritual determination to carry out what we already know, regardless of the personal consequences. Truth is a matter of life or death—what we are willing to live or die for. Can anything express the truth if it is not lived? Does truth float around as a disembodied concept? As Søren Kierkegaard saw it, much of what is publicized as Christianity is simply "poetry"—the real has been turned into the imaginary. True Christianity is turning the possible into the actual. This is the role of the prophet, to challenge us and call for obedience to the word of the Lord. This is why the Christian life is a subjunctive life. Our own feelings and desires have to be replaced and indeed redeemed if we are to enter into the indicative or prophetic reality of Christian life. Moses' words have haunted me most of my life: "Would God that all the LORD's people were prophets!" (Num 11:29 KJV).

Therefore, an inverse dialectic does not just involve us debating with each other. (It is God debating with us,) as Job was finally forced to recognize. It is not just understanding the faith, but living it out within the daily vicissitudes of personal relationships. Speculation and existence, understanding and action, poetry and prophecy, the earthly and the eternal—all of these uneasy tensions express what it means to "become a Christian" in an ongoing process. It is not enough to express personal convictions and principles. We can remain in a Gnostic or Cartesian iron cage by merely thinking about the faith and making cognitive claims for our principles.

As Jonathan Edwards realized, true affections for God are gracious affections, for they are divinely implanted in our hearts by the Holy Spirit. During the religious revival in which Edwards was engaged, too many emotional outpourings were being attributed to God when they were merely forms of psychological release. Likewise, we can speak of our Christian convictions and principles only as graciously given us in God's Word by his Holy Spirit. We did not create them, nor can we naturally will to receive them. Indeed, in sharp contrast with Platonism, we cannot assume the truth is innately within us, ready to be disclosed by speech. Rather we can express the truth only when it has been imparted personally to us by God's Spirit.

Nor are such convictions and principles given to us simply because we call ourselves Christians. They develop as God calls us personally by name. The cost of this process is the experience of being solitary, for before God we are primarily alone. Our relationship with God does not at first unite us with our fellows; it separates us. Therefore as Christians we are never more our true selves than when we are most "in" Christ Jesus. There our personal uniqueness is caught up in the reality of God's love for us, and only then does the Christian life become communal. The more assuredly we are in Christ, the more decisively we will do what the truth calls us to do. Our uniqueness and our growth in holiness go together. On the other hand, the less sense we have of our unique identity in Christ, the more indecisive, compromising and shallow we will be, and the more we will accept the popular consensus. We will remain content in the crowd, following what others do and behaving within the norms of conventional morality.

THE GIFT OF BEING JOYFUL EXILES

Christians are finding themselves increasingly marginalized by the spread of secular humanism. Yet the motif of exodus has always been the reality of God's people. "For here we do not have an enduring city, but we are looking for the city that is to come" (Heb 13:14). Loneliness is an inevitable result of our uniqueness, yet it provides space in our lives for God's presence. The Christian has a unique experience of joy, for as the psalmist reminds us, in God's presence is fullness of joy (Ps 16:11). This is an endowment the crowd can never give us, the gift of the joy of personal salvation. Sometimes it is the "joy that seekest me through pain," as George Matheson expressed in his hymn "O Love That Will Not Let Me Go." This joy is not mere resignation to affliction, but a sublimation and expansiveness of soul that is deeply settled in God's love beyond the reach of sufferings. It comes as we share in Christ's sufferings as a way of life.

True joy can never be selfish, for it is a shared social reality. When what is lost is found again, as Jesus narrates in the parables of the lost . coin, sheep and beloved son, there is great rejoicing. Joyfulness gives off a health-imparting fragrance that enlivens others. The difference between joy and happiness is that joy is a transcendence of spirit in the experience of God's love, whereas happiness is a more immanent response to a conducive environment. One is life changing, the other remains fickle.

But ultimately, like the words *love* and *peace*, *joy* is indefinable, a presence that cannot be abstracted into an idea. The great theologian Karl Barth points this out:

Our starting point is the fact that life is a movement in time—the movement of continual striving and desire for small or great ends, for new or distant goals, as guided by specific ideas, wishes, relationships, obligations and hopes. Joy is one of the forms in which this movement is arrested for a moment or a few moments, not on its objective but its subjective side, in the awareness in which man experiences himself in the fulfillment of this movement.

In other words, joy is the experience of going home like the prodigal son, of fulfilling the purpose of our creation and re-creation for God's glory. At the swine trough, pain is looking at ourselves; on the journey home, joy is gazing at the Father's love. Being joyful then is the expression of our life's fulfillment as determined by God, which at various stages of our journey we stop to enjoy and be refreshed by. The experience of joyfulness is a test of whether we are going the right way to our final destination. Joy anticipates God's love. Without hope in God, we close ourselves to joy.

We can act like Scrooge and exclude joy from our wintry lives, until repentance—the awakening to love—redirects our journey into the summer season. We can create opportunities for joy through our hospitable attitudes and kind actions, as the film *Babette's Feast* so beautifully depicts. I know someone who gives china dishes to Christian couples; this person is committed to promoting hospitality in large cities, to lighting candles in dark places. The Sabbath day is another prime opportunity to celebrate the joy of the Lord. Festivities filled the religious life of Israel, and festal joy continues to imbue true Christian community. Joy is truly a socially divine reality. It must be shared; its dictum is "rejoice with me."

True joy is also expressive of righteousness. It cannot be celebrated in the loss of personal integrity. It cannot be exercised at the expense of conscience. It ultimately celebrates our fear of the Lord, what God's

Word has determined for our well-being and that of our neighbor. Our true pleasure lies in that which gives God pleasure. True joy is being Christlike, for the Father's acclamation has been given: "You are my Son, whom I love; with you I am well pleased" (Lk 3:22). The Father anticipated that the Son would fully glorify him in his Passion, and Jesus prayed that his disciples would "have the full measure of my joy within them" (Jn 17:13). This is an incredible request when we contrast it with our petty complaints and refusal to live a sacrificial life. We need the hymn of the German Pietist Paul Gerhardt to both inspire and rebuke us: "Go forth, my heart, and seek thou joy!" Hence the fundamental basis of this joy is to take up our cross and follow Jesus in his love.

It is, then, an eschatological joy we anticipate. Here on earth we get hints and glimpses of eternal joy, which causes us to ever be restless and dissatisfied with our status as mere earthlings—we have a heavenly destiny. Joy is a new way of being, of self-sacrifice, of lifting our eyes toward the eternal, of looking beyond the things of this world, of accepting our light afflictions joyfully for his sake. It is fulfilling the prayer of Jesus that we abide in the Father and the Son through the Spirit, "so that my joy may be in you and that your joy may be complete" (Jn 15:11). It is, states the apostle Peter, "an inexpressible and glorious joy" that though you and I have not seen Jesus Christ, we believe in him (1 Pet 1:8).

LIVING ON THE DANGEROUS EDGE OF THINGS

But we still live in this world, on the dangerous edge of things. Soon after it was released in 1948, Jacques Ellul's book *The Presence of the Kingdom* helped me see the liveliness with which God's presence can enter into all aspects of culture. It turned my shallow mindset of seeking to escape from the "worldliness" of a few taboos into a desire for a redemptive encounter with the world's problems. Our Lord prayed not that the Father would take us out of this world, but that he would preserve us within it.

If Christians have no engagement with the world, then its future is bleak. We need to be sober and watchful, not seeking "solutions" but rather changed lives that can change the world. Only then can we introduce a new awareness of God's presence. A sinful world is a messy world, full of inconsistencies and uncertainties that get overlooked when we generalize theoretically about our "Christian worldview." Rather, we live in a "life-world" that is comprehensive, contingent and full of apparent contradictions.

When the poet Robert Browning spoke of "the dangerous edge of things," he was referring to a fear of paradox, an inability to see more than one side of a person or situation: "the honest thief, the tender murderer, the superstitious atheist"—and, we might add, "the popular Christian." Utilitarian philosopher Henry Sidgwick was Browning's Victorian contemporary, and there was a jest that "he never could distinguish between the kind of contradiction that was just a contradiction and the kind that was a vehicle of the profoundest truth." His was the fear of an ideologue, a fear that any breakdown of traditional thought would breach the dike and flood the world with new and dangerous ideas. Perhaps many "isms" grew out of the dread of revolution, as the French Revolution remained a raw memory in the Victorian age.

Analogous to the French revolution is our current fear of postmodernism, which has engendered a flood of skepticism. Indeed, postmodernism is associated with a far more radical revolt against God than what took place in the late eighteenth century. So the Christian today walks on the narrow edge between too rigid and doctrinaire a faith and a skepticism bordering on nihilism. Yet contemporary culture can challenge us positively to demonstrate the vitality of the gospel in fresh ways.

Perhaps it has always been difficult for devout Christians to hold truths tenaciously but with flexibility. It was easy for nominal Christians like Tennyson and Browning to blur the distinction between saint and hero, viewing Christianity itself as heroic and holding a naive optimism about its progress. For us today, any countercultural critique will be un- popular. In that sense we continue to live "on the dangerous edge of things" when we dare critique religious populism today. For the unreality of contemporary popular religion in North America is perhaps greater now than it was even in Victorian England.

What then do we lean on when we live on the dangerous edge of things? Dante leaned on Beatrice. Robert Browning leaned on Elizabeth Barrett. Matthew Arnold leaned on Marguerite, as expressed in *Dover Beach* when the melancholic withdrawal of "the sea of faith" left "no certitude, nor peace, nor help for pain." The poet could only respond, "Ah, love, let us be true to one another!" The assumption is that if you fall into doubt, then falling in love is an antidote. Better still, a woman's love may lead you to God's love. Personally, that has been my blessed experience for more than fifty years of marriage to my beloved Rita. Perhaps the boundaries between human and divine love can act as a bridge between mental skepticism and faith.

Today, with sexual and gender issues so confused and society so prone to divorce, many Christians have to live differently on their own dangerous edge of things. When male and female are homogeneously equal in public life, with no sense of biblical complement, the demand for equal rights becomes totalitarian and develops into a monotonous "each man/woman for himself/herself." When we are forced to live on the narrowest edge of self-dependence, relying only on the isolated self and seeking to live confidently in our own functional identity, it is easy to fall into despair. We begin to discover how elusive the "self" is. As in Ibsen's play *Peer Gynt*, the perennial question today is, "Who am I? What is my real self?" If our hidden formula to be a "self" is exposed and punctured like a balloon, do we fall into our own abyss? Do we live with boredom—the antithesis of joy—and accept an unexamined, superficial or

even meaningless existence? Or do we awaken from our dreams to try to
reconstruct another answer?

Since the great disjuncture brought about by the Second World War
and the apocalyptic fears of the Cold War, many people live in a montage
of cut-up discontinuities. They channel-surf with no sense of time's continuity, experiencing only shattered fragments that are inconsequential
and make the idea of "history" archaic. Perhaps the current literary renaissance of biography—and there are excellent biographies being written—reflects a cultural need for continuity and a cohesive environment
that is no longer evident. The collapse of standards and convention of
any kind makes economics our natural destiny, rather than the serious
pursuit of moral character.

Our immediate past seems to be a great chasm separating us from previous history. As novelist William Golding observes, "Belsen, Hiroshima
and Dachau cannot be imagined. . . . Those experiences are like black
holes in space. Nothing can get out to let us know what it was like inside.
. . . We stand before a gap in history, a limit in literature." New genres
and literary experiments seem necessary: literary stories, personal stories, historical narratives, poetic intuitions, meanings, myths and jour-
nalistic reports—all to convince ourselves that reality has not become a
black hole in space.

Certainly to dwell on such shadows of foreboding and uncertainty is
to live dangerously on the edge and seems more suited to the hero than
the saint, for we identify the hero with peril but the saint with joyous
peace of mind. But Christians who know themselves to be sinners can
never conceive of themselves as heroes! Graham Greene, the Catholic
novelist, tried to do so, presenting his fascination with flawed yet idealistic characters in his writings. Perhaps he was describing the divided
loyalties that develop in our lives from childhood. And today, our cultural pursuit of "Christian leadership" may represent another spurious

effort to make the Christian faith a heroic enterprise.

But it is also living dangerously to write in a confessional genre. It is a balancing act between what must remain hidden in my own soul in trust to God and what can be made public to encourage others. We can think of our life as like a musical score, appreciating what Elgar wrote at the foot of his composition *The Dream of Gerontius*: "This I have seen and heard; this is me!" Likewise in the composition of our faith, we need to confess, "This is what I have lived; indeed, this is who I now want to be."

THE RHETORICAL PERSUASION OF LITERATURE

As you will see in the following essays, I have found that great literature can enlarge our horizons concerning the human condition. As Werner Jaeger has pointed out, artistic expression "alone possesses the two essentials of educational influence—universal significance and immediate appeal." It has the power that the Greeks called *psychagogia*, the expression of the sublime in luminosity, symbol and a superior order of being. In no way should this eclipse the basic and unique importance of the Scriptures. But with the familiarity of biblical authority there can grow a narrowness and moral complacency that needs to be challenged by the cultural complexities of human life. Poetry, literature, drama and art can help us explore these complexities, just as Jesus spoke in parables to challenge the moral complacency and conventional values of his times.

Direct assertion and dogmatic affirmation can become mere religious chatter that does not shock and challenge us as we may need. Kafka wrote to his friend Oskar Plook in 1904, "I think we ought to read only books that bite and sting us. If the book we are reading doesn't shake us awake like a blow on the skull, why bother reading it in the first place?" If it is only to make us happy, then we could find happiness more readily in other diversions. No, he concluded, "a book must be the axe for the frozen sea within us."

Identification with literary characters can reveal more comprehensively the full moral consequences of our own choices and actions. They are often spelled out in narrative and biographical form in a way that fits into our own personal situations. We may see the need to exorcise our own demons by seeing them depicted in the characters of the story. At the same time, literary escape into the plot helps us see how hard it is to face ourselves directly; the indirect approach—like the parable—can challenge us from behind our defenses.

Narration helps us reflect on the mistakes of others and warns us not to repeat them. As Turkish novelist Orhan Pamuk writes in *The White Castle*, "You cannot embark on life, that one-off coach ride, once again when it is over. But if you have a book in your hand, no matter how complex or difficult to understand that book may be, when you have finished it, you can, if you wish, go back over the beginning, read it again, and thus understand that which is difficult and, with it, understand life as well."

If God could use an ass to speak to Balaam, perhaps he can use a novel to teach us to accept life-changing events. A novel by William Golding helped change the whole course of my Christian service. And I'll never forget the prophetic confrontation I experienced in reading Dostoyevsky's *The Brothers Karamazov*. I read the novel twenty years before the fall of the Berlin Wall, and I became convinced then that Marxist ideology could never last. Yet it was written a generation before socialism arrived in Russia.

In the novel, the older brother, Ivan, represents the future socialist engineer of Soviet society who believes that Christianity is harsh and theoretical. In contrast, the saintly elder Zosima communicates a very different picture of Christian life, one that is tangible and personally real.

As Dostoyevsky wrote to his publisher:

> I will force [the Russian socialists] to admit that a pure and ideal Christian is not an abstraction but a tangible, real possibility that can be contemplated with our own eyes, and that it is in Christianity alone that the salvation of the Russian land from all her afflictions lies.

It is a message we still need to hear today.

PART 1

Christian Faith as a Way of Life and a New Identity

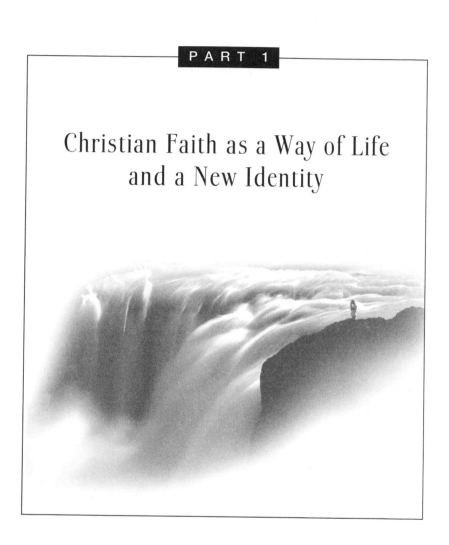

The Breath of the Hidden Life

Set your minds on things above, not on earthly things.
For you died, and your life is now hidden with Christ in God.

COLOSSIANS 3:2-3

Where I am most inwardly myself, there You are far more than I.

AUGUSTINE
Confessions

It is the juxtaposition of contraries, i.e. union without reconciliation,
that defines the underground in all its aspects.

RENÉ GIRARD
Resurrection from the Underground

*A*nimals have the ability to use camouflage to hide themselves from predators. Many humans attempt to hide themselves from God, assuming he is a cosmic predator. In sharpest contrast, our humanity requires that we deliberately exercise hiddenness to avoid the temptation to rival God. The desire "to be as God" *(eritis sicut Dei)* is a perversion at the core ✓ of our being; it is the refusal to be truly human. This is the meaning of sin—the perversion of our imagination and actions to be anything but creaturely. Sin is never content with being "hidden with Christ in God" (Col 2:3), for our creaturely condition requires humility as we stand under the Creator's way of being. Our sinful temptation is to seek superiority over others, to want equality with God, to try to make religious "deals" with him, to insatiably desire conspicuous glory.

Instead of being amazed at the condescension of God to become human (Phil 2:6-7), perhaps we should define our humanity by God's interpretation of what he intended humanity to be—in becoming human himself he practiced self-emptying humility, living in perfect obedience and dependence on the Father. He emerged from the poverty of the crib in the manger to a hidden life of thirty years in the carpenter's shop. He even allowed people to misunderstand much of his three final years of public life. He was not the Messiah of nationalist expectations. He was the antihero. Yet as we shall see, such a hidden life is the breath of the gospel.

Without an awareness of the hidden Messiah, our instinct to hide is motivated by a desire for self-protection. We want to conceal ourselves from physical danger, as when Moses' mother hid the child in the river to protect him from Pharaoh's slaughter of firstborn Hebrew boys (Ex 2:1-10). Likewise, Rahab hid the spies and David hid from the wrath of Saul. This instinct to hide grows out of the vulnerability of poverty and destitution; as Job observed, "The poor of the earth hide themselves" (Job 24:4 KJV).

We also hide morally, out of shame, as when our first parents "hid from the LORD God among the trees of the garden" (Gen 3:8). The shameful barrier of sin isolates all humanity from God. As Isaiah states, "Your iniquities have separated you from your God; your sins have hidden his face from you, so that he will not hear" (Is 59:2). Frequently in Scripture God is said to have "hidden his face" because of the Israelites' unbelief and rebellion. Could it be that God also hides from our neurotic attitudes? When we ask, "Why is God not hearing and answering my prayers?" perhaps it is because such prayers distort the character of God.

There is a universal awareness, even in primitive religions, that humans cannot understand the divine by ordinary perception. A veil of mystery envelops divinity. This numinous shroud is even more impenetrable in contrast with our own mortality and the reality of death. Yet the Greeks devoted their entire culture to exposing and explaining the inscrutability of nature. They did this originally through heroic mythology, breaking down the boundaries between the human and the divine. In the Olympus myths the hero is more than human, born of divine parents and capable of pursuing the superlative quality of excellence (*arēte*)—heretofore the province of the gods. Perhaps our technological society is another "heroic" culture, extolling human achievement and applauding exhibitionism and pride. It is only the awareness of death that sobers us, the knowledge that eventually we will be permanently hidden within the earth. Only the sculptured monuments of marble bodies will remain in defiance of such an end to our mortal bodies.

THE BIBLICAL THEME OF HIDDENNESS

The Old Testament, on the other hand, is distinctly antiheroic. It imparts an awareness of the infinite separation between Creator and creature. God is holy—literally, the "wholly other." Thus all that belongs to God is hidden from us. The closer we think we are to approaching God, the more vast the distance becomes. The Eastern church fathers perceived this truth: what we acknowledge we don't know of God contains far more of his mystery than what we think we know of him. God's character is self-revelatory. He alone can reveal himself, for nothing is hidden from him. Sinful man flees from such divine omniscience, but when judgment falls, there are no rocks in which to hide from his wrath (Is 2:10; Jer 4:29). Yet the righteous need not hide from his presence (Job

13:20). Rather, wise is the one who hides God's Torah as a treasure within himself (Prov 2:1).

Likewise, the New Testament takes up the theme that the things of God are hidden, notably with regard to the kingdom of God. It is like treasure buried in a field (Mt 13:44). It is like leaven that disappears in the dough (Lk 13:21). Jesus reiterates frequently the need to keep the messianic realm secret, for those who are blind and deaf to its teachings cannot receive it. Inevitably, revelation remains closed where there is no receptivity. Even the disciples could not understand Christ's Passion (Lk 18:34). Significantly, after Jesus told the people what "kind of death he was going to die," he "hid himself from them" (Jn 12:33, 36). Likewise almsgiving, prayer and fasting should be practiced in secret so that the heavenly Father who sees the secrets of the heart may award appropriately (Mt 6:4, 6, 18). As the poet W. H. Auden expressed it, "To a Christian the godlike man is not the hero who does extraordinary things, but the holy man who does good deeds. But the gospel defines a good deed as one done in secret, hidden, so far as it is possible, even from the doer, and forbids public prayer and fasting in public."

Jesus roundly condemns theatrical religious showbiz. The gospel of John shows that Jesus did not make a public impression during much of his life on earth, for the messianic message had to be concealed (Jn 7:4-6). Again from Auden: "It is impossible to represent Christ on the stage. If he is made dramatically interesting, he ceases to be Christ and turns into a Hercules." Yet the Christian message must be communicated, for it is not a hole-in-a-corner affair. This generates significant tension for Christians, knowing when to speak and when to keep silent. The Christian life has nothing to hide, yet its efficacy is bound up in being hidden from the world. The incarnation cannot be seen by the world, only by the eye of faith.

A significant Scripture text regarding the hidden life is Colossians 3:3:

"Your life is now hidden with Christ in God." In context Paul is describing the consequences of being a Christian. Our lives have to become analogous to Christ's life, contingent on what he experienced. He died, then rose again from the dead. So it is only in Christ that the new life given to us can reshape and transform us to be Christlike. Only in his death and newness of life can we receive it. Only in such hidden inwardness is our new self reborn. It implies a spiritual death.

The father of German Pietism, Johannes Arndt, first used the expression "to die to" in German, and then Kierkegaard adopted its Danish equivalent, *at afgo*—a rarely used verb meaning "to die away." Hiding ourselves when the world tempts us to exhibit ourselves is an effective way of "dying away." Satan presented to Jesus the temptation to cast himself from the pinnacle of the temple in a heroic act of exhibitionism, yet he chose to stay hidden within the will of his Father. This too is Paul's idea when he challenges the Christian believers: "Since you died with Christ to the basic principles of this world, why, as though you still belonged to it, do you submit to its rules?" (Col 2:20).

The Colossians were being tempted to follow false teachers who denied Christ's sole divinity and claimed that humans were demigods, proudly and ostentatiously substituting the self for God. Create your own religion, they said, speculate about angels and, like New Age spirituality today, substitute yourself for God. In sharp contrast, the apostle urged believers to remember that they had died with Christ, that they must now seek a selfless way of living. This is what "hiding" is all about—denying the world's ways, making choices that are incomprehensible to anyone seeking self-fulfillment. Indeed, it is refusing to accept Satan's cosmic suggestion that "you will be like God." It is the deepest longing of man to ascend to the divine, to be like God. But it is this that we must die away from most of all. We cannot achieve this process wholly in this existence, so it remains a present participle—we are "dying away" throughout our earthbound existence, and it requires a continuous hiding.

We can place a stronger emphasis on the hiding of the Christian life if we restate the Colossians verse to read, "You died and your life is now hidden with the Messiah in God." Jesus of Nazareth was the hidden Messiah, living obscurely in Nazareth; contemporaries of Jesus asked the question, "Can any good come out of Nazareth?" Considered an itinerant and homeless teacher by the common people, he never trained publicly as a rabbi or belonged to a guild like the scribes or Pharisees. He entered Jerusalem on an ass's colt, yet he was the King of kings. He was lifted up not on a throne, but on a cross between two thieves. Truly the gospels depict him as antiheroic. Inevitably, then, Christians must partake of the hidden life of their Messiah. Is it any wonder that if he was not recognized, many will not appreciate our hidden life? What can the followers of the Messiah expect other than to cause offense and stumbling when Jesus himself caused scandal among the leaders of Israel? The Christian life is truly scandalous to the world.

In Luke 14:26 Jesus challenges his disciples, "If anyone comes to me and does not hate his father or mother, his wife and children, his brothers and sisters—yes, even his own life—he cannot be my disciple." Jesus was addressing large crowds in previous verses, but he makes this statement to an individual. That is to say, communication is personalized only when it is individuated, "hidden" in our own heart.

A student who grew up in a loving Christian family recently told me, "I just prayed that one day, the explanation of this verse would be made clear. I have waited a long time for this to happen." Like it is for so many of us, "love" was more a feeling than a way of life for this young woman, and "hate" was more a negative than a positive. Nor had she realized that "loves" may signify possessions (Lk 14:33) rather than relationships. Family loyalty was the norm of conventional morality in the society Jesus addressed; it was expected of everyone.

Biblically, the word *hatred* implies not so much a feeling as a mode of activity, similar to *love*. Jesus is not telling us to cultivate emotional dislike of our relatives. Rather he is urging us to eschew nominal morality that is unreflective, popular, hereditary and habitual, involving no conviction or commitment. To be a disciple of Jesus is an intimately personal decision to abandon all else in order to follow and obey him exclusively. The foundation of Christian discipleship is to hate all constraints that would keep us from supreme loyalty to Jesus. The messianic revolution demands full allegiance only to him, even at the cost of hating our own life. As John 12:25 puts it, "Those who love their life lose it, and those who hate their life in this world will keep it for eternal life" (NRSV). A hidden life involves self-renunciation. It is the exercise of the deepest form of interiority, of relinquishing all that would impede us from Christ being formed in us.

Being hidden in Christ, dying away, and even hating nominal morality all reflect the same reality. Suffering, sacrifice, self-denial and mortification are all expressions of this life that is "hidden with Christ in God." Certainly, Colossians 2:6—3:4 expresses the apostle's radical opposition to all externalized, manmade existence, whether secular or religious. But he goes on to assure us that although our life remains hidden, it is securely preserved in God. God is the secure place in which to be hidden, for it is he who is unseen (Col 1:15). Elsewhere Paul affirms that Christ is his life (Phil 1:21), and "I no longer live, but Christ lives in me" (Gal 2:20).

Of course, this double identity creates much tension in our Christian life. In Romans 7, Paul draws the distinction between the inner and the outer man, confessing, "In my inner being I delight in God's law; but I see another law at work in the members of my body, waging war against the law of my mind" (Rom 7:22-23). This duality is not between body and soul, as Plato saw it, but between willing and doing. Also, more critically, it is a temporal difference. We read in Paul's prayer of Ephesians 3:16-17, "That out of his glorious riches he [the Father] may strengthen you with power through his Spirit in your inner being, so that Christ may dwell in your hearts." Paul also explains in 2 Corinthians 4:16, "Though outwardly we are wasting away, yet inwardly we are being renewed day by day."

This is the new eschatological existence of the Christian; we have a future that must be allowed to develop even though it is not fully manifest. It remains hidden because it is "not yet." The newness is still invisible externally, but it is truly there. It entails freedom from the tyranny of sin and the passions and death, but alas, it is not yet fully expressed. So the new person still sighs under the bondage of the external life, still struggles, as Paul still cries in pain (Rom 7:24) and sighs under his burden (2 Cor 5:4). True, the inner life is not visible enough, but nonetheless it is real, more real than any external mirrors we use to reflect on the ways of the world.

AUGUSTINE, THE APOSTLE OF INWARDNESS

All of us stand on the shoulders of our forebears, so to reflect on inwardness is to reflect on Augustine, who first stressed the importance of the inward way. Augustine (354-430) begins his *Confessions* by remarking how strange it is that human curiosity impels us to explore distant lands, to climb mountains, even to probe the depths of the oceans, which are all external things. Yet how little self-understanding we have, and how little concern for the inner life before God. If Augustine is known as *Homo Viator*, "Man the Traveler," he is above all the explorer of the soul. No serious Christian thinker has failed to be influenced by him. Indeed, he may be called the founder of Western consciousness since he so enlarged the inner Christian life. His doctrinal battles with the Manichees, then with classical neoplatonism and also the Christian heresy of Pelagius, all extended his Christian horizons widely. But it was his meditations on Scripture in self-understanding that helped him recognize the inner self. It was the realm where one could find God. As he states, "Where I am most inwardly myself, there you are far more than I."

This is in sharp contrast to the contemporary psychological self, where the more you know yourself the less you need God. Instead, like Plotinus and many other classical philosophers before him, Augustine takes self-knowledge to be the first crucial step toward the knowledge of God. As he prays in his *Soliloquies*, "Let me know thee, O God, let me know myself, that is all." In turning inward toward the soul, we turn upward toward a higher being. Augustine recognizes the soul's ability to look in, and then up. The first stage in this process is turning away from "bodies," or external realities, toward interiority. The second stage is contemplative, gazing up toward the beauty of God in his uniqueness as the source of all intelligence, truth and beauty.

However, unlike the pagan neoplatonists—and indeed, our own contemporary versions of the inner self—the privacy of Augustine's interior life is not private property, in irredeemable and unbridgeable solitude. Rather it is common to all souls. God is for all humanity, and truth is to be communicated and shared by all. So the communion of saints shares an inward unity; all are bound together by the love of God. Heaven will be the sphere where we can all share each other's inmost thoughts without hindrance. Privacy in the inner life is a mark of the Fall, of the presence of sin in our lives. Instead, we should be wholly transparent to each other, with no barrier to divide and separate us. Being able to express ourselves to others, with all kinds of signs, gestures and behavior, was as vital for Augustine as it is in our own inner life. This expression helps us integrate inner and outer, soul and body. Moreover, unlike the contemporary frame of mind where the soul is wholly surrendered to the sensate life of the body, Augustine saw the soul and body like two chariot horses pulling in harmony of motion in the same direction toward the same purpose.

In the late Middle Ages, when major socioeconomic changes were influencing the stability of monastic life and institutionalization of the religious "hidden life," the church sought a recovery of Augustinian balance. Benedict had taught that monastic life should be both "prayer and work," *ora et laborare*. But merchant burgers and their wives in Flanders and the lower Rhineland promoted a new synthesis as *devotio moderna*. It focused on the urban home as a domestic convent for communal prayer and Bible study.

English Augustinian canon Walter of Hilton writes about the need to exercise "the mixed life," active and outer as well as inner and contemplative, as symbolized by Martha and Mary both living in the same house. Walter also added the symbol of Lazarus, risen from the dead. The apostle's proclamation, "your life is now hidden with Christ in God," can only be true in the context of death to the self and life to God, as Lazarus symbolizes. There can never be a true unity of soul and body, or of inner and outer life, without our unity in the death and resurrection of Christ.

THE REFORMATION AND THE INWARD LIFE

The Puritans inherited this focus on the hidden life as the sphere of family devotions, and also the monastic emphasis on meditative silence. Silence is certainly one aspect of the hidden life. But from the Reformation they also inherited an awareness of the self-deception intrinsic to the natural human being. The Puritan Thomas Brooks has given us a classic on this ambiguous discipline in *The Mute Christian Under the Smarting Rod* (1659). His focus is on Psalm 39:9: "I was silent; I would not open my mouth, for you are the one who has done this," and he begins by warning us that "we are the greatest snare to ourselves." He then notes

several false motives for silence, including stoicism, political motivations, sullenness and despair. Alternatively, he notes that true silence is
gracious and holy, always keeping God in sight. The seven qualities of
this godly silence are as follows:

1. We recognize God's presence even in affliction.

2. Once we have gained some understanding of God's holiness, we obey
   the injunction to "Be silent before the Sovereign LORD" (Zeph 1:7). Ps 4:4

3. With further experience of God's grace, we rest submissively and
   peacefully in him, never blaming him for our afflictions and declar-
   ing, "I know, O LORD, that your laws are righteous" (Ps 119:75).

4. The conviction grows that "in all things God works for the good of
   those who love him" (Rom 8:28). This helps us in deepest trust to
   leave the outcome wholly in his hands.

5. We are constantly reminded that it is not God's character to afflict un-
   necessarily; it remains "his strange work" (Is 28:21).

6. It becomes easier to listen to God's command: "Be still before the
   LORD and wait patiently for him" (Ps 37:7).

7. Finally, such wise and trusting silence before God becomes saturated
   with his presence, so that willingly we surrender and resign ourselves
   into God's gracious hands, murmuring, "Speak, LORD, for your servant is listening" (1 Sam 3:9).

In this process we leave behind the city lights in order to go deeper
into the wilderness to appreciate the stars of the night sky. So too we
learn to cultivate silence and solitude in order to have a clearer vision of
the character and ways of God, for we still see through a glass darkly. The
inward life is still what T. S. Eliot called the path of "observance, discipline, thought and action. The hint half guessed, the gift half understood."

A solely outward existence tends to live by secondhand opinions and attitudes that we never assimilate personally within our own hearts. Instead, we need Mary's posture, hiding the living Word within our heart to become pregnant with the Word. Instead of living on the social circumference of externals, we need the hidden depths of a centered life, learning to distinguish between the inner and outer, between God and the world, between the Holy Spirit and our spirit. Even then we need to question interiority, to discern God's Spirit from our own temperament and narrative, as Thomas Brooks has hinted.

THE DANGERS OF INWARDNESS WITHOUT CHRIST

Inwardness has always been a natural part of my life. As a child I was sickly, a missionary kid and the only boy, and I grew up with much emotional insecurity. Later, in my professional role as an Oxford tutor, I was directed not to public lectures but to the intimacy of the tutorial system. Listening for many hours each week to my students' essays became a way of life, which developed later into other contexts. I chose to be a spiritual mentor instead of a public fund-raiser for my institution, concluding that I could not ask others for money if I desired to nurture them intimately in Christ. So the hidden life cost me a more visible career and became a lifelong journey. It led me down paths of personal faith rather than institutional success.

Yet without Christ the hidden life can be dangerous! With greater interiority there can be greater self-deception. We may assume we have a conscience like an implanted pacemaker in our hearts, but then we discover "the conscience" is more of a Greek than a biblical concept. It can deceive us into thinking we have always been "good people," but later in life we may discover it has suffocated us. All this shows how much we live on the circumference rather than from the center of our being. We may miss true inwardness entirely, and our shallowness leads to distorted thinking about ourselves and God| Our own introspection proves to be the wrong compass by which to navigate our souls. It is only in gospel inwardness that a new self can be truly born and grow.

Prayer can certainly enhance an inward orientation when it is checked by and accountable to God. From a vantage point of prayer we learn to observe more clearly the external arena of the world, whereas the self seeks to establish itself and build itself up in its own sufficiency. ✓ It considers impressing others more important than pleasing God. It is affected by the toxic disease Richard Rohr calls "affluenza," which has such(a blinding and shallowing effect on our existence.) Prayer then is not just a spiritual discipline, needful as this may be. Rather, prayer expresses existentially this hidden life before God in adoration and thanksgiving as the appropriate relationships of inwardness toward eternal love.

But we need guides and companions on the way into the hidden life, otherwise it can be too rigorous a journey. I have found both Kierkegaard and Dostoyevsky to be remarkable guides. As few others, they complement each other in exploring the depths of Christian experience. Both explore the inner life with great seriousness as the place of greatest ambiguity. I shall always remember the radical freedom I first sensed as I began to read Kierkegaard's writings about the human condition before God. And just as Augustine affirms the need of a life companion concerning the double knowledge of knowing ourselves in the light of knowing God, so also Dostoyevsky's *Notes from Underground* depict living in the cellarage of our own undisclosed and sinful motives.

INTERIORITY IN KIERKEGAARD

Perhaps no greater Christian thinker in the last two centuries has exemplified more profoundly the need for our life to be hidden in God than Søren Kierkegaard (1813-1855). Shyness, melancholy, irony, even frivol-

ity were all natural covers for his inner life. Like an effective spy in enemy territory, he both camouflaged and truly hid his life before others.
He wrote sermons but did not preach them. He did not want the gospel
to be passed by, and the preacher may expose himself to being readily
dismissed. He wrote under pseudonyms, so his reader is always uncertain who is saying what and why. Indirect communication, as our Lord
himself used in parables, reaches us more subtly, and also perhaps more
intimately. We need to understand the truth for ourselves and not have
it imposed on us abstractly.

Inwardness involves dread when we sense the vacuum of loneliness
and even of nothingness. In "The Concept of Anxiety," Kierkegaard bril-
liantly explores the effect sin has on our inner lives, since with the loss
of God there is also a loss of self. He anticipated what secularists today
are recognizing as the "lightness of being." In the loss of transcendence,
immanence becomes trivial, even banal. In contrast, a favorite theme of
Kierkegaard's is that "against God, we are always in the wrong." Such a
realization will always help us attend to our inward life.

In many of his works, Kierkegaard interprets three stages of human
consciousness. The Christian has to grow through and overcome these
stages in order to appreciate the divine relationship. It is instinctual to be
"aesthetic"—that is, to live only on the surface of things. We need to die
away from the aesthetic stage in which we habitually exhibit ourselves
like Hollywood stars—showing off our bodies, our intelligence, our accomplishments and our passion for happiness and living impatiently in
quest of instant gratification. No wonder such worldly aesthetes have
such fragile and brittle identities, fostered by narcissistic personalities in
a narcissistic culture. The cure lies in our ongoing dying away to all these
things, in learning the importance of a hidden way of life.

Second, there is dying away to the moral life. This is subtler, for moral
activism can be blinding. It is a Pelagian type of righteousness that is

zealous for good works yet uses the "tools" and "techniques" so beloved of technological society. In this stage all our efforts to live as good people remain self-achieving, and the results have nothing to do with the gospel. It is the life lived by modern-day scribes and Pharisees. Today, many institutional Christians are morally respected because of what they do for the church, but they don't understand that in the hidden life in Christ it is "not because of righteous things we had done, but because of his mercy" that he saved us (Tit 3:5).

Kierkegaard cites Abraham's test by God as the supreme example of dying away to the moral life. As a result Abraham has been misunderstood ever since. He stood on Mount Moriah with the knife poised over his only son Isaac, ready to slay him as a sacrifice to God. His motive has remained so hidden since then that controversy still rages over how his obedience to God could ever be thought morally acceptable. The father of the faithful, Abraham's faith still cannot be understood as humanly moral.

Third, there is the stage of human religious consciousness. Kierkegaard claimed to be a "prophet of the second Reformation," setting himself against the national Danish church to advocate that Christendom needed to die if the reality of true Christianity was going to be reborn. But he would have told you that if you were called to be such a prophet, you would need to place yourself outside the establishment and be ignored. All favors and rewards of ecclesial life must be resigned by anyone who would call it to repentance. You cannot be a leader and a reformer of the church at the same time. John the Baptist had to accept being a voice in the wilderness to lead the renewal of God's people. This was his exercise of the hidden life in order to proclaim the advent of the Messiah.

Dying away to religious life means being rejected—and hidden indeed. Kierkegaard had longed to be a parish priest in the Danish church; instead he never preached his sermons, he only wrote them. Only the in-

dividual reader can understand how personal it is to become a Christian
with a truly hidden life. Kierkegaard also used irony to communicate indirectly. As he put it in *Sickness unto Death*, "When death is the greatest
danger one hopes for life; but when one learns to know an even more
frightful danger, living a lie, one can only hope for death." How great
then is the despair when one cannot die, knowing that the despair of the
soul is sin, not death.

Likewise, how many of us as Christians experience death to our own
self-made identities in order to receive a new one from Christ? Kierkegaard helps us take the first step in this direction. "God wants dissimi-
larity, lack of conformity with this world." But he adds, "Ah, we who still
call ourselves Christian are from the Christian point of view, so pam-
pered, so far from being what Christianity does require of those who
want to call themselves Christian, dead to the world, that we hardly ever
have any idea of that kind of earnestness." For when he speaks of "earnestness"—a key word in his writings—he means that to be a true Christian, we need to have death as our teacher of earnestness. Kierkegaard
perceived that we often popularize Jewish piety, which says that the
closer we are to God the more blessed we are, whereas in the Christian
life the closer we are to God the more we may suffer. Ironically, then, it
is easier for a non-Christian to become a true Christian than for a nominal Christian to achieve this same reality. Without Christian earnestness,
Kierkegaard argues, we can have no essential reality. The individual's life
then becomes impersonal, whereas such earnestness helps deepen our
Christian subjectivity and to possess the faith for ourselves.

Let us then focus on being rather than doing. As we do so, we will
experience a growing earnestness that never dies. Also, accepting misunderstanding meekly will help us turn more inwardly to God, to "taste
and see that the Lord is good." As Kierkegaard puts it, "Christianity is an
existence-communication," appropriated before it can be shared. So si-

lence and solitude are required in the assimilation of Christianity before we communicate it to others. No flowers can grow in the garden without roots in the soil. Or, to use Jesus' imagery, there can be no fruit unless the branches abide in the true Vine.

THE FALSENESS OF THE UNDERGROUND PSYCHE

A life hidden in Christ is not the same as going "underground." This is the message we learn in reading Fyodor Dostoyevsky (1821-1881). He was a generation later than Kierkegaard, and from his Russian context he also feared the Enlightenment embrace, but more specifically he warned against socialism with its abstract and alienating ideology.

In *Notes from Underground* (1864), a prelude to his great novels, Dostoyevsky is no longer content to rehash his old certainties and to justify himself in his own eyes. He had spent four years in prison and five more exiled in Siberia. He had become a true Christian, yet he remained haunted by pride. His self-achieved realism could still push him over the edge into anarchic individualism rather than reconciling grace. For the rest of his life Dostoyevsky would live in the ambiguity of Romans 7, in the duality of faith and pride. His was an underground psychology that could endure great personal affliction yet remain mixed with a greedy diet of flattery and self-absorption.

From his exploration of human nature in *Notes from the Underground,* whose hero is nameless, Dostoyevsky now writes *Crime and Punishment.* The hero of this novel is Raskolnikov (*rask* means "schism" or "separation"), who is a self-portrait of the author. He is a solitary dreamer, trying fiercely to test the limitations of his existence, not knowing whether he is a god or an earthworm. So he lives with these two personae. Money and eroticism both play significant roles in his existence as part of the "will to power," which later fascinated Nietzsche in reading this novel. The idea is that if you are nothing in the eyes of the world, be everything in your own eyes. (Nietzsche would further argue, don't just dream about it, do something about it as the Superman.)

But compensatory behavior of any kind never gives life to others, for it causes us to act as our own saviors. Ironically, it is frequently our compensatory behavior that brings us the world's accolades. The girl that was never noticed storms the theatrical stage with acclaim; the lonely boy turns inwardly to books to become a great scholar; the butt of the teacher's ridicule becomes a powerful business consultant; the outsider in the schoolyard becomes the famous novelist. The dynamics of the underground psyche are, however, always the same—they do not satisfy the hungry heart, nor do they give life to other people. Pride rules in place of God, and we think we do not need divine grace. The "underground" is literally "the room below the floor," our psychic unconscious where neurotic drives and passions rage and where thoughts flourish that are not brought under captivity to Christ. Later, for Freud, this was the sphere that became the substitute for God himself. For him, the subconscious lacks the ability to analyze and moralize, whereas for Dostoyevsky, as in *Crime and Punishment,* the subconscious is deeply moral. Thus the dreams and impulsive actions of Raskolnikov struggle against his rational mind's rejection of moral values. What Edgar Allan Poe had called the "perverse," Dostoyevsky now calls the "paradoxical," and this becomes a major instrument in his exploration of the human psyche. The modern loss of transcendence does not eliminate the spiritual world, but as Dostoyevsky saw clearly, the displacement of God brings in the demons instead.

When living in Christ, we need the humility of discernment to distinguish the true hidden life from an underground life of alienation. The reality is that we are created as relational beings. But as sinners our perversity is to relate enviously rather than lovingly. In envy we desire possession; in love we surrender. So role models prompt our instinctual proclivity to imitate. When, however, our role model is wise and good, then appropriate desires are directed heavenward instead of remaining underground. For with Christ there can be no conflict of interest and no rivalry; as our mediator between God and man, he is uniquely our Savior, indeed the Lord of all creation. As René Girard observed, we go underground when our mimetic desires are frustrated. Then the underground hero finds "he is as selfish as he can possibly be, and this is precisely where his trouble lies: he cannot be sufficiently selfish. His intense mimetic desire compels him to gravitate around human obstacles of the pettiest kind."

Girard concludes that "mimetic desire is a realistic theory of why human beings cannot be realists." In a world as empty of transcendence as ours has become today, people left to their own devices will tend to choose the underground. Where there are no transcendental signposts, we can trust only in our own subjective experience, becoming "little Cartesian gods with no fixed reference and no certainty outside ourselves." For as Girard further notes, mimetic desire is failed selfishness. It is then we live with despair as our inmost companion—unless we recognize with the poet George Herbert that we can live with two contrasted dimensions. As a friend of Charles I in the early seventeenth century, Herbert was a courtier, a public orator of Cambridge University, very much in the public eye. Yet he renounced it all to hide as a country parson, shaping his life as he shaped his poem (note the progression of the italicized words; emphasis added).

> *My* words and thoughts do both express this notion.
> That *Life* hath with the sun a double motion.
> The first *Is* straight, and our diurnal friend,
> The other *Hid*, and both obliquely blend.

One life is wrapt *In* flesh, and tends to earth.
The other winds toward *Him*, whose happy birth
Taught me to live here so, *That* still one eye
Should aim and shoot at that which *Is* on high:
    Quitting with daily labor all *My* pleasure,
    To gain at harvest an eternal *Treasure*.

Being Open to a
Visionary Life Before God

I tell you the truth, you shall see heaven open,
and the angels of God ascending and descending on the Son of Man.

JOHN 1:51

O King Agrippa, I was not disobedient unto the heavenly vision.

ACTS 26:19 (KJV)

Am I not free? Am I not an apostle?
Have I not seen Jesus our Lord?

1 CORINTHIANS 9:1

In an age of busily creating our own professional identity, I found it refreshing some twenty years ago to meet with Henri Nouwen. As someone who followed a path of downward mobility similar to my own, he left Yale and Harvard in exchange for the l'Arche community to nurture the mentally handicapped. We laughed together about the misunderstandings such a move created among our colleagues. As I mentioned in the last chapter, I have long been inspired by the voluntary transformation George Herbert made from royal courtier to country parson. Not all are called to do something so radical, but these examples continue to challenge us about our own ambitions as Christians. For we lose credibility when we use Christianity as a "career."

∦   Our natural tendency is to maintain earthly values and to resist focusing on our heavenly destiny. Sacrificial life is intrinsic to the Christian faith, for it presents a constant demand to choose between higher and lower values. Moreover, sacrifices are usually by their character irrevocable, although when they are made for our loved ones and friends, we have some tangible satisfaction in seeing them benefit. But when our sacrifice is for a heavenly destiny, then we have to live by faith and not by sight.

THE CHARACTER OF CHRISTIAN VISIONARY EXPERIENCE

To my knowledge neither Henri Nouwen nor George Herbert had what we might call a mystical experience. But Blaise Pascal (1623-1662) certainly did. As the mathematical genius who invented the first calculating machine, he was sitting in his home on the evening of November 23, 1654, reading the Gospel passage about Peter's thrice-repeated denial of Jesus at his Passion. Pascal saw himself in Peter's denial, and wept much. He looked at the clock, and noted all this had happened precisely between 10:30 p.m. and 12:30 a.m. So he went to his desk and wrote a profoundly moving record of his experience, calling it *The Memorial*. Ever after he wore it sewn into the inside of his cloak. No longer was his God an abstract notion of philosophers, but the God of Abraham, Isaac and Jacob, the personal God who can enter our heart and commune with us as friend to friend.

✓Christian mystical experiences are just that: personal encounters with the living, revelatory God. One moment, like Peter, Pascal was in desolation and darkness, and the next moment he was delivered into the light of the fiery love of a forgiving and accepting God. Certitude, joy and peace filled his being in the contemplation of the risen Christ who, he wrote, has become "my God and your God" (Jn 20:17). Pascal found that renunciation and forgetfulness of the world brings nothing but "joy, joy, joy, tears of joy!" It is having "everlasting joy in return for one day's striving upon earth."

Pascal is not alone in this joyously divine encounter. We remember Augustine's *Confessions* and the narration of his conversion experience in the garden. We reflect on many more encounters: Francis of Assisi called to rebuild the ruined chapel, Julian of Norwich's visions of her suffering Lord, John Newton's rescue from both the sea and his own sinful life, Simone Weil's awareness of her acceptance by Christ in the Eucharist— and indeed the experiences of a great cloud of many witnesses. To encounter God in our lives is to encounter his love, even though that love may be challenging in its transformation of our self-will and enlargement of our human desires.

WRESTLING WITH GOD

This kind of encounter is illustrated in Jesus' call to Nathaniel to become his disciple. Jesus saw him "under the fig tree" (Jn 1:48)—an allegorical expression of the limited cultural expectations Nathaniel shared with his contemporaries regarding the Messiah. It suggests that Nathaniel was living with a small, self-focused horizon, content to remain as a "good earthling." From his self-interested perspective, he could only wonder whether any good could come out of Nazareth. Jesus responded to his limited earthbound desires by extending his horizon, promising that Nathaniel would witness God's presence in this world by seeing Jesus Christ transcend earth and heaven as sovereign of the heavenly host. Jesus promised him, "You shall see greater things. . . . You shall see heaven open, and the angels of God ascending and descending on the Son of Man" (Jn 1:50-51).

Clearly this was an allusion to Jacob's dream, when he saw a staircase

up to heaven on which the angels of God ascended and descended. In
√ the Old Testament, dreams were readily interpreted as the undefined territory between the human and the divine. They were the contact zone
between the natural and the supernatural. Today, dreams are interpreted
as illustrating the depth of human personality. Together, these perspectives indicate that even in dreams God can reach down to us and penetrate the very core of our being.

√ We should not discount the need to be open to God, even in our
dreams. Dreams guided the Patriarchs (Gen 15:12-21; 20:3-6; 28:11-22;
37:5-11; 46:2-4), and later Gideon, Samuel, Nathan, Solomon, Zechariah
and Daniel all had significant dreams. In the New Testament Joseph had
important dreams (Mt 1:20; 2:13, 19, 22), and Paul's nocturnal visions
were significant to his ministry (Acts 16:9-10; 23:11; 27:23). But just as
there are false prophets, so also there are lying dreams, which are frequently condemned (Deut 13:2-5; Jer 23:25-32; Zech 10:2). And it is clear
√ that dreams are always of secondary importance to the revealed Word of
God, which has supreme authority in the conduct of our lives. It is worth
noting that all visual dreams in the Bible require interpretation, as if to de-
note the primary authority of the Word over psychic visions of any kind.

Jacob's two dreams are central events in his own narrative. The first
one at Bethel, which Jesus referred to in speaking to Nathaniel, occurred
on the eve of his departure from the Promised Land to the foreign land
of Laban. It was an assurance that God's presence would be with him
(Gen 28:12). But Jacob's power, which enabled him to accomplish exceptional tasks such as lifting the heavy stone off the community drinking well, appears to have tempted him to remain a prayerless giant. So
God allowed him to experience many frustrations over the next fourteen
years, including the temporary barrenness of both his wives, Rachel and
Leah. In fleeing from Laban, he has to face his angry brother, Esau. It is
just before this fearful encounter that he has his second dream, wrestling

with the angel in the darkness of the night and receiving a dislocated hip that leaves him crippled (Gen 32:22-32). In other words, he has to be broken in order to change his identity and truly become Israel. Then no longer is he a powerful and cleverly autonomous supplanter, but one who has seen the face of God.

As a college student in Edinburgh, I took many a cold lunch on a wintry day in the public park near the National Art Gallery, feeling depressed and living a dislocated life. Years later I entered the art gallery to see Gauguin's famous painting of Jacob wrestling with the angel. Paul Gauguin (1848-1903) painted this work in 1888, calling it *Vision after the Sermon*. It depicts a foreground of Breton women circled in prayer at an annual festival of confession. In the center is depicted the imaginative wrestling match between Jacob and the angel, representing the women's inner imagination while they listen to the sermon by the priest, who is in the right corner of the picture. Gauguin is using this theme to demonstrate his break from Impressionism, which was the prevailing art form in the Paris salons. He places this scene defiantly in Brittany, the most conservative religious environment of France, to proclaim a new and revolutionary art form.

It is also clearly autobiographical, with Gauguin himself the wrestler. He wrote four years after the painting was completed to his friend Daniel de Monfreid: "You are right, my friend, I am a strong man who is able to bend fate to my desires; I can assure you that to do what I have done in the last five years [i.e., challenging Impressionism] has been quite a *tour de force*. I'm not talking about my struggle as a painter; yet that counts enough—but about the struggle for life, with never a stroke of luck in my favour!" He adds that the best way to win in this struggle is to take a day at a time, as a wrestler "who doesn't move his body until the moment he starts fighting."

Thus in spite of the religious theme of his painting, Gauguin is really describing the secular Darwinian struggle of the survival of the fittest, not divine intervention as Jacob experienced. Gauguin wrestled with no angel. He never changed his name, and he never received a new identity. Instead, he left his wife and five children to pursue his own career. His movement of postimpressionism launched self-expression and anticipated what we now call New Age spirituality, in which the hubris of the human spirit leaves no space for God's presence in our world.

I now look back gratefully on my youthful years of brokenness as a divinely given asset, not a defect. Again and again, the words of 2 Corinthians 7:10 have comforted me, as paraphrased by J. B. Phillips: "The pain that is borne of God has an effect too salutary to regret." Limping through life may not be such a bad thing after all!

Like the Bretons of Brittany, the republic of Georgia also has a long tradition of wrestling. Recently, I was in Georgia and met a two-time national wrestling champion. He explained to me why the sport suited the national psyche, hemmed in as they were in the narrow mountain valleys and in poverty and isolation. Indeed Stalin, a Georgian, was a fierce political wrestler and the whole world trembled before him. Yet we all wrestle: in self-will, in the fierce passion to get our own way, in pride. Connative intelligence—that is to say, the ways we balance willfulness and will-lessness in wise willingness—is a poorly developed discipline of the soul before God. This is one of my own most significant struggles, seeing that my will may not be God's will for my life. We can easily forfeit a visionary life before God in our pride, because it is only the pure in heart who see God.

OPENNESS TO OUR OWN MORTALITY

An effective way to become open to the ways of God is to reflect on our own mortality. At my age, I do it increasingly! But at whatever age we are, young or old, we miss a lot if we refuse to practice "death-awareness." We cannot do this by viewing death with objective detachment. Rather we need to accept the inevitability and unpredictability of our own death as subjective truth. Our secular culture would have us deny anticipation of death, with the consequence that this repression leaves us with a shallow view of our own selfhood. But if we can live with a constant awareness of death, we will treasure all the more deeply that our identity is committed eternally into the hands of God for safe-keeping. How richly secure we become with this assurance, as the apostle shared with Timothy, his son in the faith (2 Tim 1:12).

Kierkegaard, in the third of his *Three Discourses*, urges us to cultivate seriously a truthful sense of death-awareness. He describes how an old man he had known was enriched in every part of his life by this death-awareness, seeing everything relative to eternity.

> He recollected God and became proficient in his work; he recollected God and became joyful in his work and joyful in his life; he recollected God and became happy in his modest home with his dear ones; he disturbed no one by indifference to public worship, disturbed no one by untimely zeal, but God's house was to him a second home—and now he has gone home.

So Kierkegaard does not see mortality as a source of morbidity and despair. On the contrary, he interprets a true awareness of death in God's presence as a source of joy, infusing our life with vitality and genuine appreciation of God in all circumstances. We can pray, "This may be the last day of my life, Lord, so help me make the very best use of it for thy sake. Amen." Death then can become "the teacher of earnestness." Again, as Kierkegaard says in *Sickness unto Death*, "When death is the greatest danger, we hope for life; but when we learn to know the even greater danger [i.e. moral death], we hope for [metaphysical] death. When the danger is so great that death becomes the hope, then despair is the hopelessness of not being able to die."

That is to say, there are three contrasted situations. First, for those who see death as the terminus of all earthly existence, they desperately want to go on living as long as possible.

Second, for those who fear moral deadness more than bodily mortality, the metaphorical Christian death is the option they choose. In the death of Christ, the Christian understands that death is not the final end; indeed it is a passing into life. Dying daily in Christ provides the vitality we need for new life in Christ. Our natural personality needs to be freed to allow the life-giving Spirit to slay us so we can re-live in Christ. (Otherwise, in spite of all our knowledge of Christian doctrine, we shall continue to grovel miserably in selfishness and avaricious attachment to earthly values and possessions.)

Third, there is the tragic state of suicidal despair, in which someone seeks only annihilation. Without the risen Christ, death is seen as a one-way journey with no return to the state of mortals. Without Christ, death might mean the release of the soul from the body to a state of immortality. It might imply transmigration of the soul. It might even usher one into a state of divinity, as later Roman emperors believed. For the early Hebrews, it was Sheol—a state of next to nothingness. "No one remembers you when he is dead. Who praises you from the grave?" (Ps 6:5). It was forbidden for the Hebrews to try to make contact with the dead, as Saul tried to do with the witch of Endor (1 Sam 28:3-25). Only later does Scripture speak of hope for those "who sleep in the dust of the earth" (Dan 12:2-3), based probably on Isaiah 24—27.

But in our Lord's time, the Sadducees ridiculed the idea of resurrection as well as the Pharisees' identification of departed souls with an angel or spirit that went on living. Thus throughout history, the resurrection has been a revolutionary doctrine.

Paul's earliest letter, 1 Thessalonians, salutes those who have "turned to God from idols to serve the living and true God, and to wait for his

Son from heaven, whom he raised from the dead—Jesus, who rescues us from the coming wrath" (1 Thess 1:9-10). Then later, Paul elaborates on the hope of the resurrection for Christians, now dead, who will be "caught up together with them in the clouds to meet the Lord in the air" (1 Thess 4:13-18)—changed indeed! The resurrection, too, was part of Jesus' promise to Nathaniel, that he would see greater things. As modern-day Nathaniels, sometimes we experience this desire for life after death as a deeper longing than we ever imagine could be fulfilled. Through our love of God, the door of perception in faith becomes enlarged and we "see heaven opened," henceforth accepting that God is always greater than our imagination, desires or expectations. To speak trustingly in God is to be open not to what is above us and inaccessible, but to what we can experience right here and now. One moment we can be living under a fig tree, and then we see an open heaven far beyond our wildest dreams!

As we have seen, Kierkegaard fears moral death more than physical death. By "moral death" he means the religious and moral illusions that we may engender by living with generalities such as "Christianity is the state church" or "Christianity lies in its past." These must be exposed just as Nathaniel's false messianic expectations needed exposure. But, to quote Kierkegaard, "the matter of getting rid of 1,800 years as if they had never been," is like questioning Nathaniel how long he can remain dwelling under his "fig tree," that is, under his falsely construed messianic hopes. These had to die if Nathaniel would see the Messiah for who he is, even as one coming from Nazareth, a "no place" on the Israelite religious map. Only living within proximity to death allows a person to reflect on the truth of one's finite humanity in utter dependence on God. Nathaniel's ground for belief could not rest only on a prophetic past, but on the presence of Christ who is always present. Nathaniel accepted the invitation to "come and see," as we also must continually do. Then, "seeing the heavens open," we are prepared for God's unfolding revelation, even for the ascension of Jesus itself.

THE ASCENSION AS EXPRESSIVE OF GOD'S OPENNESS

Jesus' ascension into heaven was made possible by his sacrifice on the cross. He was the Lamb of God offered up on our behalf. The uniqueness of his priestly act destroys all other religious cosmologies, for the Lamb that was slain now stands before the throne and rules forever and ever. Jesus was crucified under Pontius Pilate more vividly than Mel Gibson's *The Passion of the Christ* could possibly depict. Forty days after his resurrection from the dead, he left the disciples in the ascension, which they all witnessed. From that point on, Christ's incarnation, death and resurrection, ascension and Pentecost are all inseparable, determining the course of history and reordering our own cosmologies. As Irenaeus suggests, our anthropology as humans is really God's story of what it is to be created in the image and likeness of God. In this story our eyes are opened to see Jesus Christ as the ultimate expression of God's glory. "The heavens are opened wide"! That is why the late John Paul II never tired of interpreting human history as "God's story."

The theologian Jürgen Moltmann has helpfully distinguished the terms *future* and *advent* in the way we see God in our world. "Future," as the Latin word *futurum* denotes, is what will or may come to be based on the past and the present; it connotes cause and effect. "Advent," or *adventis*, implies a manifestation of the future coming into the present and changing what the future will be. "Grace and peace to you from him who is, and who was, and who is to come" (Rev 1:4). That is say, God's future is not in what comes to be, but in he who comes into our world.

The Greek word *physis* (Latin *natura*) has no eschatological significance. These terms are material; "physics" and "nature" can reflect only an organic "coming to be" of that which is already present in embryo.

In this classical mindset, Hesiod speaks of Zeus who "was, and is, and will be"—that is, will be in the future as he was in the past. But in sharp contrast, Isaiah proclaims messianically, "Prepare the way for the LORD" (Is 40:3), and then John the Baptist exclaims, "Look, the Lamb of God, who takes away the sin of the world!" (Jn 1:29). It requires only a change of slant to see the difference. As Ray Anderson puts it, "Effective ✓ leadership means reading the signs of God's promise in the context of present events and translating these signs into goals; this is 'preparing the way of the Lord.'"

In Christian ministry, I have experienced many defeats. Not getting our own way is imprisonment; it is living in the desert; it is exile; it is a form of death. And yet we find, wonder of wonders, that this barrenness can become fruitful, ushering in a transcendence of life that was previously unimaginable. It becomes the advent of God into our life.

Long ago, as a teenager, I received a green plastic text I kept on my student desk: "Them that honor me, I will honor" (1 Sam 2:30 KJV). This was a favorite text of Eric Liddell who was a generation before me in Inter-Varsity circles in Edinburgh. Throughout my life I have believed that this is true. One honor that I experienced vividly, yet have rarely shared with others, was in fact the most transforming of my Christian experience. Why has it remained hidden? Most of my Christian friends would be embarrassed about its disclosure, or at least cautious about making it public. As a close friend advised recently, tread gently! Revealing it here is a bit like saying, "I believe in angels, and actually I saw one yesterday in the garden."

Public opinion allows us to read *A Rumor of Angels* by Peter Berger and recognize "signals of transcendence." Billy Graham also assures us that we can believe in their reality. But to *see* them? As Gregory of Nazianzus once said, our minds go into a spin at trying to find the right way to speak about the elusive nature of angels. Yet angels form part of the incarnation and resurrection narrative that is pivotal to the gospel message. Judeo-Christian belief left open, especially in first-century theology, the range of description for "prophets" as God's servants and "angels" as God's ministering spirits. Diversely, they both served God. The former were seen as humanly embodied communicators of the word of God, the latter as expressing the glorious presence of God as pure spirits.

In Exodus, there is also ambiguity between the words *angel* and *cloud*: "The angel [Hebrew *mal'ak*] of God, who had been traveling in front of Israel's army, withdrew and went behind them. The pillar of cloud [Hebrew *'anan*] also moved from in front and stood behind them" (Ex 14:19)—i.e., both to guide and also to defend them. Perhaps Stephen is referring to this tradition when he declares explicitly that Moses "was in the assembly in the desert, with the angel who spoke to him on Mount Sinai, and with our fathers; and he received living words to pass on to us" (Acts 7:38). When, then, is a cloud an angel, or when is the man of God also an angel?

CHRISTIAN MYSTICAL EXPERIENCE IS UNIQUE

In 1961 and 1962, my family spent a pleasant sabbatical year in Winnipeg, our first visit to North America. I had taken part with a large group of students at the InterVarsity Urbana Mission Convention at the end of the year. Just after my return I was awakened one night by an incomparable light at the foot of my bed. Strangely, I did not feel curious about what I was seeing, but I experienced an inner conviction deeper than any I have had before or since that I was in the presence of God. No voice spoke, but I knew beyond all telling that I was being called to surrender myself wholly to whatever God wanted to do with my life. I responded similarly to Saul of Tarsus, saying, "Lord, what will you have me to do?" Like Samuel, I invited God to "speak, Lord, for your servant hears."

I waited eight years wondering what that commission might be. Then I received the call to leave Oxford, my professional career and our native country for a new endeavor in Vancouver, British Columbia—the founding of Regent College. In many times of stress and suffering that visionary nighttime experience has brought joy and certainty that our family was called irrevocably to commit our future to Regent and its community.

During the early years of the college we experienced numerous events that unbelievers might call "remarkable coincidences," each strengthening our family's conviction that the hand of the Lord was on this crazy venture. One just doesn't begin a new academic institution with four students and a pile of financial debt expecting to become affiliated with a major secular university in four years. My children interpreted these events as divine intervention, even though they were only teenagers at the time. Many of Regent's faculty and students have likewise experienced the presence of God in certain events, although none have necessarily shared my own night encounter. So what is the place of a visionary life in the Christian faith? Why are we wary of mystical experiences?

Such encounters with God remain positive and lasting in their influence. A Christian couple I know met when the young woman had long been distrustful of all men. Her father was an alcoholic and had left her family at a young age. But when she met her future husband, my friend had a mystical experience, seeing God embrace her and this man together in his arms in a sweep of trust. The circle of the embrace, however, was not quite complete; it was broken off at the ends and seemed to sink into a void. The marriage lasted more than twenty years until her husband became unfaithful, leaving his wife brokenhearted yet with remarkable inner strength. She interpreted the original vision as an assurance that God had always been in their marriage and would renew it at a future date. Her friends cannot understand her indomitable spirit, but she has met with God more than once, in apparently remarkable ways, and trusts him wholly as Immanuel.

At the beginning of the twentieth century, spiritual revival within the religious establishment was associated with renewed interest in Christian mysticism. The rise of the Pentecostal movement occurred then also, and various new forms of religious experience became prevalent. Looking back, we may interpret this era also as a cultural reaction to the rationalism of the Enlightenment, which had suppressed the human spirit in its emphasis on thinking rather than living. The word *mysticism* was coined early in the Cartesian revolution in reaction to its rationalism.

The Roman Catholic church has been more open to mysticism, because the idea of natural theology (knowing God the Creator by natural reasoning) and of God's revelation by grace opened itself to a third category: mystical theology. This development was based on certain saints' experience of God's presence with peculiar personal intensity. Evangelical Christians reject this threefold approach, asserting that only divine revelation enables us to know God, not nature nor mystical subjectivism.

Karl Barth, for one, raised serious theological objections. He challenged even the great Augustine's experience, shared with his mother Monica at Ostia, as contradicting the orthodox understanding of divine revelation. Does mystical experience not threaten the objectivity of God's acts through the distortions of human subjectivity? Does it not make the mystic the bearer of revelation and thereby deny the transcendence of God's dealings with us? Yet even Barth admitted grudgingly that mystical experiences are not wholly alien to Christian thinking, provided they are grounded in the experience of the indwelling Christ.

We are not to deny the supernatural life Christians are given by God and called on to live. But our own human spirit does not have the potency for direct access to God. We do not need to train as contemplative athletes to attain special mystical knowledge. Like every other human

endeavor and achievement, mysticism should be viewed with awareness
of its ambiguity and its questionable nature. Ironically, those most hostile about it may not think to question their own intellectual prowess!

We cannot doubt that God is fully capable of entering into the personal life of his disciples in ways of his own choosing. But we are more inclined to live habitually in the comfort of institutional Christianity than to be vulnerable to God's personal intervention in relating with us. This openness can seem very threatening, even death-giving—which of course it is, as we saw earlier. The recipient may find that a mystical encounter is experienced at a level deeper than ordinary exercises of worship and prayer. It may therefore be indescribable in its uniqueness and assessed as sublime. It is no coincidence that in its vested interests the institutional church has always viewed the mystical life of individuals with suspicion. For how can the uniqueness of personal Christian relationships be held in balance with general consensus—let alone church bureaucracy!

Yet the greatest mystics wisely caution us not to overemphasize mystical experiences themselves. These men and women have always affirmed that the message is more important than the messenger. For John of the Cross, as well as for Teresa of Avila, Julian of Norwich and Francis of Assisi, there was no question of indulging in mystical experiences for their own sake. They all witness to the validity of their experiences by the ethical effects on their lives and their promotion of Christian growth. The experiences boldly affirm the reality of the living God. The fruits are in the powerful effect such reformers of the faith have had, and continue to have, on the life of the church. So John of the Cross, the great Spanish mystic, cautions us that such "rare occurrences, of which few have had experience, seem for these very reasons the more marvelous and the less credible . . . and so people will think that it is not in itself as great a thing as it is."

Language cannot exhaust our personal mystical experiences of God, as T. S. Eliot reminds us:

Words strain,
Crack and sometimes break, under the burden,
Under the tension slip, slide, perish,
Decay with imprecision, will not stay in place,
Will not stay still.

√   When we have had a special experience of God that we can only describe as mystical, the test of its validity is our personal response and its benefits to ourselves and to others.

As Colin Thomson notes, modern culture can be cruel toward systems of consciousness other than our own. Liberalism is generous to our own intellectual system of thought but rigid and even bigoted toward those of the past. So to be prejudiced toward the Christian mystics is to be intolerant of a different form of human consciousness. Neurophysiologists tell us that we all have a simple core consciousness with a generic sense of self. But beyond this level there are complex layers of extended consciousness related to past memories and experiences and feeding into an ever-expanding personal matrix of entities, events and values. Dorothy Sayers once wrote in a letter, "I am certain it is desperately important to get the mystical and poetic approach to life accepted naturally at an early age or when the mind is uncorrupted by rationalization." And Reinhold Niebuhr once said, "Every child is a born theologian," asking questions only the mystical life can deal with. Augustine speaks of this consciousness as the rich inner mansion of memory, which we shall explore later.

THE OPENNESS OF THE NEW TESTAMENT TO THE OTHER

From my own intimately personal mystical experience has come the lasting conviction articulated by Paul: "Am I not free? Am I not an apostle? Have I not seen Jesus our Lord?" (1 Cor 9:1). I cannot claim the role of an apostle who has physically seen Christ Jesus, but we can all become apostles in the root meaning of the word: one who is sent as a representative. So our freedom is one of obedient willingness to be sent by God, motivated by a personal experience of Christ. But before we claim too hastily an affiliation with Paul's attestation, perhaps we should explore, first of all, what Christian consciousness looks like in the New Testament.

Human consciousness was more porous in the past than we now experience. Rationalization since the seventeenth century has tended to close us within ourselves, and this process is reinforced by our technologically driven desire to "fix things." But the New Testament narrative of angels, miracles, exorcisms and apocalyptic dreams suggests that the boundaries between spheres of reality were more fluid in late Antiquity. As Klaus Berger has noted, the biblical-era mentality carries "a pronounced openness toward the dimension of the Other; indeed, manifestations of the Other are expected. . . . The Other is no longer sealed off from the past but rather has become a latent feature of the present, a possibility lying just under the surface. The same holds true of eschatological realities, wonders, visions, and new revelation." Miracles were signs of another realm where God reigned supremely. Thus the demythologizing efforts of liberal scholarship result in a refusal to accept the New Testament consciousness. We have to ask ourselves whether we judge the experiences of others according to our own limited experiences or from a transcendent perspective, such as may be considered according to the purposes of God.

The biblical-era perspective was less individualistic and self-contained, less attentive to feelings, less a body-soul dichotomy that ignored the soul than our own contemporary consciousness. The permeability of the self left key New Testament figures open to the presence of Moses, Elijah and John the Baptist, indeed to the presence the risen Christ

and his work in us. Freedom was viewed in a radically different way: not
as the liberty to do what we want but as freedom *from* things—from death,
from sin, from self, indeed from our own secular skepticism—to love, to
obey God and to show love for others. Paul interprets the Christian life as
one of vicariousness, of experiencing the atoning death of Christ, of inter-
ceding in prayer for others and in suffering on behalf of the gospel.

As Christians, the Corinthians felt free to indulge in their "rights" on
the basis of knowledge (1 Cor 8:1-6). They knew the idols were fake, so
eating the meat offered to them was no big deal. But this offended the
conscience of less mature believers and threatened to divide the community. In this context, the apostle became a personal example of subordi-
nating rights for the good of the whole church. Because he was sent of
God as an apostle, he was certainly no less free than the Corinthians
thought they were, but like his Lord before him, he renounced his rights.
On the Damascus road he had seen his crucified and risen Lord, who
had freely loved even unto death. Later on trial as a prisoner of the state,
his words rang out: "O King Agrippa, I was not disobedient unto the
heavenly vision" (Acts 26:19 KJV).

With the Damascus road encounter filling his whole being, how
could he continue to persecute the body of Christ? These words, then,
sum up the meaning of mystical experience for every Christian: obedience, freedom and the vision of Christ.

All the mystical events of the New Testament are connected to one
historical person: Jesus of Nazareth. Just as some of us are fearful or
skeptical of the mystical, so were the disciples when they saw Jesus
walking on the water. As he drew near to them, they were scared (Jn
6:19), but when they let him into their boat they experienced beneficial
results (Jn 6:21). Only God can walk on water, or indeed subdue the
storms of life or overcome the cosmic abyss. By accepting him in Christ,
we can experience the same freedom as the disciples to overcome every

storm of life, every threat of death. But since a mystical experience of Christ is a result of God's presence, it remains incomprehensible. The only response can be faith and not doubt. As Berger says, suggestively, "Faith is one's persistent engagement in the efficacious reality of God." It is imaginative yet carries a prayerful confidence in a trusting relationship that dissolves the sense of "I alone" for "we together."

Faith is also a transformation that takes place in the midst of ordinary life and its domestic affairs. In the New Testament shepherds are tend-ing their flocks in the fields, a wedding is taking place in Cana of Galilee, fishermen are out in their boat, Saul is traveling on the road to Damascus. But translated into another state of being, life can never be the same again. Old perceptions are refocused by new conceptions of life and its relation-ships. We become alienated from the ordinary, break through barriers and no longer believe a description of God but God himself.

Some of our greatest literature expresses this open-ended sense of multidimensional reality. The medieval symbol of John's Gospel was the eagle, for his message soars above our horizons, drawing us out of our self-centeredness to abide with Jesus in the eternal Father's bosom. Jean Vanier aptly entitled his meditative study of the gospel *Drawn into the Mystery of Jesus.* Jesus is the heart of the mystical life, giving us new di-mensions to explore. In him we do not take flight from our world, but reenter it with a divine mission: to love people as Jesus loved them.

We think of how Dante leads us with the help of his two guides, Virgil (reason) and Beatrice (Christ's love), to explore hell, purgatory and heaven. John Bunyan had to dream in order to narrate *The Pilgrim's Progress.* In our day, Charles Williams has disclosed in his novels *Multiple Dimensions, Descent into Hell* and *War in Heaven* the proximity between the natural and the supernatural. Like his friends J. R. R. Tolkien and C. S. Lewis, as well as Dorothy E. Sayers, he is convinced that the spiri-tual world does not merely parallel the material world, but rather serves as its source and abiding infrastructure. We humans do therefore make significant choices with eternal consequences. So when we shut ourselves up in our own narcissistic projections, no longer able to love or, as Charles Williams puts it, to coinhere, hell is the veritable result. Long before Lewis became a Christian, he had already observed:

> We need no barbarous words nor solemn spell!
> To raise the unknown. It lies before our feet;
> There have been men who sank down into Hell
> In some suburban street.
> And some there are that in their daily walks
> Have met angels fresh from the sight of God.

THE RELEVANCE OF ANGELS

Biblically, the worship of angels is forbidden. Yet we are commanded to give heed to them as messengers of God, for their presence is God's presence, and their actions are his actions. Their purpose is to reveal the will and thoughts of God. As the writer to the Hebrews asks, "Are not all angels ministering spirits sent to serve those who will inherit salvation?" (Heb 1:14). While they are not restricted by space or time, being neither corporeal nor incorporeal, they minister at the boundaries between heaven and earth as the messengers of God.

Angels turn up at decisive points of the gospel narrative. They appeared to Zechariah, the father of John the Baptist, forerunner of the messianic kingdom (Lk 1:11-25). Gabriel spoke both to Joseph and the virgin Mary to announce the advent of the Messiah (Mt 1:20-25; Lk 1:26-38). The shepherds heard the angelic chorus in the fields around Bethlehem (Lk 2:9-20). The angels strengthen Jesus in his temptation in the wilderness and at his agony in the garden of Gethsemane, as well as at the empty tomb (Mt 4:11; Lk 22:43; Jn 20:12). And at his ascension, two angels told the disciples that this same Jesus would come again in the way they had seen him ascend into heaven (Acts 1:10-11).

As T. F. Torrance wrote in an essay honoring my seventieth birthday, there is a "spiritual relevance of angels" for those of us who are in the covenant life of God. They bear witness to the heavenly realm that is our destiny. In being mindful of our pilgrimage, they keep us open to our heavenly destination. They confront us in the Bible, reminding us to keep its holy character in a holy way. They entreat us to accept the Scriptures as having a divine origin beyond our comprehension. As Torrance writes, "If the heavens are open as the angels ascend and descend on the Son of Man who is the incarnate Word, we must surely approach and interpret the written Word of God in a similar manner, for in their own appointed way the Holy Scriptures constitute the ladder of communication between earth and heaven on which there constantly ascend and descend the heavenly messengers sent out to help us lift up our hearts and minds to God in spiritual communion with him." Through its role in mediating the awesome presence of God in our lives, the Bible becomes both the house of God and the gateway into heaven.

When I was recently engaged in an inquiry into how Christian colleges could enhance their quality of chapel worship, too often the request was made for more funding for musical instruments. When the choir director has a doctorate of worship and noted musicians give musical performances that draw theatrical applause, it is time to reintroduce angels as ministering spirits. For angels are the worshipers par excellence! George Herbert recognizes this in his poem *Miserie*:

Lord, let the angels praise thy name.
Man is a foolish thing,
Folly and Sin play all his game. . . .
My God, I mean my self.

This thought echoes Hebrews 1:6, "Let all God's angels worship him," for as the conveyors of God's Word and the messengers of the divine will, angels are worshippers in a superlative capacity. Though prominent in the beginning of Old Testament revelation, angels are especially active surrounding the incarnation in the New Testament. Thus the birth of Christ was heralded cosmically by "a great company of the heavenly host . . . praising God and saying, 'Glory to God in the highest, and on earth peace to men on whom his favor rests'" (Lk 2:13-14). Angels are also prominently featured with the new order brought about by the resurrection.

John the seer also records the heavenly liturgy hymned by the angels, which is echoed by the Eucharistic liturgy of the church: "Holy, holy, holy is the Lord God Almighty, who was, and is, and is to come. . . . You are worthy, our Lord and God, to receive glory and honor and power, for you created all things, and by your will they were created and have their being" (Rev 4:8, 11). And they sing "a new song" to the Lamb: "You are worthy to take the scroll and to open its seals, because you were slain, and with your blood you purchased men for God from every tribe and language and people and nation. You have made them to be a kingdom and priests to serve our God, and they will reign on the earth" (Rev 5:9-10).

This echoes the trisagion of Isaiah 6:3: "Holy, holy, holy is the LORD Almighty; the whole earth is full of his glory." But whereas Isaiah saw the Lord "high and lifted up" on a throne, John saw "a little lamb that was slain," for he had been high and lifted up on a cross, as John 12:32-33 states in deliberate contrast. So "the song of Moses the servant of God and the song of the Lamb" (Rev 15:3) are deliberately conjoined as the united testimony of both Old and New covenants. Human expectations and divine interventions are united in such visionary expectations, the latter correcting the former.

Likewise, Calvinists need Gregorian chants and Catholics need to chant the Psalter, with some angelic assistance necessary for both parties. Otherwise our worship tends to become traditionally inverted, even ethnic. It is the role of angelic ministry to open our ears and eyes ✓ more widely to the visionary splendor of the Lamb who sits on the throne, uniting all the nations of the world in a blending of the visible and invisible, so that things become not as they appear. We expect kings to reign, not a slain lamb, and for our ego-centered institutionalism to direct the choir, not the poor and the outcast. This is the prayer then of Richard Baxter in the seventeenth century, who first speaks of being the "mere Christian":

> Ye holy angels bright,
> Who wait at God's right hand,
> Or through the realms of light
> Fly at your Lord's command,
> Assist our song,
> Or else the theme
> Too high doth deem,
> For mortal tongue.

DISCERNING THE MYSTERIES OF DIVINE PROVIDENCE

Even a secular novelist like Saul Bellow complains that humanity tends to cheapen mystery by "explaining everything away" like a small bird cheeping on a fence. This is no angel singing! Yet we live not only with the mystery of the Bible and of our worship, but also with the mystery of providential events that cannot be readily dismissed. A friend told me recently that once when she was driving fast on the highway, she faced an inevitable crash into a wide lorry just ahead of her, hemmed in by traffic on her left and right. Preparing for death, she closed her eyes, only to open them a few seconds later and find herself miraculously beyond the lorry and still safely on the congested highway. She has no explanation of what took place other than divine providence.

In all likelihood, Daniel could not explain how he survived in the lion's den. Jonah could not explain what happened when the great fish swallowed him up, then left him on dry land. Nor could Peter tell us how he escaped from prison. Likewise, there are occasions when we can accept a synchronicity of events only as being orchestrated by God.

In the personal narrative of Jerry Levin, CNN bureau chief for the Middle East, he tells how he was kidnapped shortly after he arrived in Beirut. As a Jewish secularist chained to a cold radiator in a dark prison cell, he began to think about faith and God. For six months he had nothing to read, but during ten intensely contemplative and spirit-filled days beginning on April 1, 1984, he began to ponder about faith, God and his fellow human beings as he had never done before. Nine months later, he realized his journey of faith had only begun.

It happened this way. On Christmas Eve 1984 at about ten or eleven o'clock, one of my captors paid an unexpected late night visit to my almost freezing cold cell. I was additionally surprised when he wished me a merry Christmas and asked if there was a gift I would like. Hardly thinking about the answer, I replied immediately, "A Bible. That'll do." I needed a Bible; because, after nine months of belief that I was quite aware I had acquired without benefit of studying scripture first hand, I was anxious to read it from start to finish. I was especially keen on knowing whether or not I had gotten it right—especially with respect to praying. To my astonishment two nights later my captor came back and gave me a brand new red pocket-sized Gideon New Testament, Psalms, Proverbs along with a ball point pen. . . .

Three days later . . . when I had got to the part about the shepherds in Luke 2:8-20—"when they had seen him, they spread the word concerning what had been told them about this child, and all who heard it were amazed at what the shepherds said to them" . . . I heard footsteps in the hall outside my unlit pitch-dark crypt-like room. That sound was the signal to me to pull my blindfold over my eyes, which I did. . . . After the man left, I pushed the blindfold above my eyes and beheld the most astonishing—or at least, unique—sight of my captivity. On the floor, anchored in a puddle of melting wax was a flickering candle. Next to it was a bowl of fruit. And next to it a big platter and on it a "log" type of chocolate cake. In front of the cake was a very intricate and beautiful Lilliputian manger scene. Intricately carved pines stood guarding a tiny wooden barn, open to view at one end. Inside was a minuscule manger. Sitting before it was Mary holding Jesus with Joseph standing close by. There were several shepherds looking on plus cows, horses, and sheep—all carefully crafted and painted in a smaller than toy soldier scale.

The passing minutes crackled with a kind of physical and spiritual energy that seemed to be dissolving the centuries separating me from the event. I actually experienced a kind of vicarious surge when I recalled that this was happening to me not too many miles to the north of Bethlehem in a frigid room that I imagined was not any colder or less comfortable than the one in which Jesus had been born. . . . To relate what we witness and try to make sense for others of that long ago event is what shepherding is all about. It is, I believe, job enough to keep us all meaningfully occupied for the rest of our lives. It is a job with no end, but every day one with a new beginning, which I gladly attempt to perform.

By virtue of the angels' presence in our lives, we can penetrate the veil of sense and unbelief to discern the invisible works of God. Angels proclaim these works when we are open to God's providing care and love. Providence and mission are both enfolded in their wings. Jesus exhorted his disciples, "Do not look down on one of these little ones. For I tell you that their angels in heaven always see the face of my Father in heaven" (Mt 18:10).

Torrance cites a story of his father, a missionary in southeast China. One day he received a letter from a Chinese man who had never heard the gospel, yet made many pilgrimages seeking "eternal life." He dreamed one night that along a mountain road he came across a stone archway on which were chiseled the words, "The way of eternal life." As he made his way through the arch, he was confronted by a man in white who asked him what he wanted. He said he was in search of eternal life. The man in white invited him to enter through the arch. In his excitement he awoke and recited his dream to a friend. In response, his friend told him he had just met a stranger who had given him a tract entitled "The Way to Eternal Life." It was written by a missionary, the father of Tom Torrance. His search was over.

While our life is "threescore and ten"—and I am now well past that—Luke reminds us that after the resurrection, "they can no longer die; for they are like the angels" (Lk 20:36). So we have an undying future. No wonder I love Paul's words: "Am I not free? Am I not an apostle [am I not "sent"]? Have I not seen Jesus Christ my Lord?" Our life to come will not be spent closed up to molder into the dust of a tomb; it will open to eternal life.

Today there are too many Sadducean Christians who do not live in the light of the resurrection and ascension of Christ. Their faces are not open to the heavens. They need to be reminded that when Moses was taken up onto the mount to receive the Ten Commandments, he was delayed so long the people got impatient. "They gathered around Aaron and said, 'Come, make us gods who will go before us. As for this fellow Moses who brought us up out of Egypt, we don't know what has happened to him" (Ex 32:1). So some ask today, "Jesus Christ—what has happened to him?" He is in heaven, still distinctly and uniquely a Man, man as God intended us all to be, so our destiny is there, not here. The ascension √ points to such a destiny and the purpose of our life here on earth. Life and death, success and failure, reality and appearance, worship and idolatry take on different meanings for us than for the world around us while we "wait for his Son from heaven" (1 Thess 1:10).

THE WORD OF GOD AS OUR STANDARD

Although we have made much reference to the Scriptures in this essay, we still need to inquire into the role of the Bible in our openness to the transcendent. It's easy to become "flaky" and credulous about everything beyond our ken. My wife Rita and I were once watching a large balloon floating over the beach at Vancouver, and I admired its spectacle in the air while she looked to find where it was attached to the ground! Snaking along from the air was a cable attached to a Toyota on the edge of the road. Solemnly she pronounced, "I am Jim's Toyota." So too the Word of God has to be both our divine inspiration and our practical anchor for day-to-day living.

As a boy I always found my Father reading his Bible, and his inattention to my own needs put me off from reading the Bible. John Muir, I found out later, had the same experience, and it sent him off alone into the Scottish highland glens to commune with nature instead of his father's God. He has become the patron saint of the Sierra Club, more a leader of environmental pantheism than of his Christian childhood. For me, Bible reading produced an emotional paralysis from which I had to ask God for release. I began to realize that there are always three versions of the Scriptures: ancient, modern and neurotic! The first two we know well, but the third can be subtle. Many Christians waste much of their devotional life trying to overcome it, especially if they have known the Scriptures from childhood. Perhaps we need a new perspective, such as Kierkegaard's discovery that the Scriptures are God's love letters to us. Or that their diverse genres reflect a whole corpus of diverse purposes in reading them. Or that they are truly our daily manna that comes down from heaven for our spiritual food.

For myself, I have found it helpful to use the Scriptures according to the phases of life. So as I lacked the discipline of meditation, I spent a whole year on Psalm 119. Each stanza of eight verses provides a meditative framework for a verse each day, with two on Saturday. As a youth I was guided to spend several years on the book of Proverbs, which I rediscovered later at a depth provided by the exhaustive devotion and scholarship of my dear friend and colleague Bruce Waltke. The Lord's Prayer was my constant reflection and guidance for four memorable years. The Beatitudes likewise were formative in constant reflection. The Scriptures have been so many guideposts on my life's journey, with the Gospels significant at one stage, the Epistles at another, the Psalms constant companions, and so on through the extraordinarily varied biblical library we have inherited. *The Parables*

Thus the more we are shaped by the Word of God, the less we are merely psychological beings—closed to the transcendent and guided by flat subjectivity. In the latter state we are not sufficiently aware of the historical and spiritual dealings of God with his people, nor can we explore deeply our own emotional life. Our human relations tend to inflate or inspire our identity, indeed to destroy or transform it. Seeing ourselves from our own point of view becomes a prison. In contrast, seeing ourselves from a biblical perspective enlarges our horizons to the solemn grandeur of eternity. Only when we glimpse the eternal can we begin to gain the "double knowledge" spoken of by the early church fathers: entering into a true knowledge of ourselves along with a growing knowledge of God.

Without the Bible, the despair of a diminishing soul is the natural consequence. We may be unconscious of such despair unless we reflect on how boredom fills our life. Or we may be willfully despairing, aware of our rebellion against God, or will-less in our despair because of weak resolve. We live daily then on God's Word to maintain synthesis between our enclosed natural life and our open, eternal destiny. That is why the virgin Mary is the true archetype of the Christian, receiving the Word of God enclosed within her natural womb and yet open, so open, to the promises of God, incredible as they might appear to all around her. She remained fully a woman, and yet becoming fully herself, she was empowered by the Holy Spirit to become God's vehicle for the mystery of the incarnation. Such a woman helps me as a man to believe also in the promises of God, that he "is able to do exceedingly abundantly above all that we ask or think, according to the power that works in us" (Eph 3:20 NKJV).

PART 2

The Priority of Personal Calling over Institutional Life

THREE

The Surrealism of Christian Public Life

Is it then the walls of a church that make a Christian?

AUGUSTINE
Confessions

*I think that if ever I become a serious Christian
I shall be most of all ashamed that I did not become one sooner,
but first wanted to try everything else.*

SØREN KIERKEGAARD
Journals

*Create in me a pure heart, O God, and renew a steadfast spirit within me.
Do not . . . take your Holy Spirit from me.*

PSALM 51:10-11

Essentially, we have seen that the Christian life is hidden from those to whom Jesus Christ is not the Son of God. It may also be hidden from our friends who are "not there yet" in their own journey of faith. Yet it is not pridefully underground, since the Christian humbly lives in openness to the mysteries of God.

Between these two spheres, we now explore an indeterminate realm between our public and personal life: organized religion. Here public religious life is rapidly losing credibility, even dying. Here people are questioning the feasibility of the Christian life because it is either not hidden deeply enough in God or it is not open enough to God. Its incredibility lies in the way it has mixed the ways of the world and the ways of the self with what it purports to be the ways of God. In its surrealism it is neither truly real to God nor realistic about humans' innate sinfulness. As Pascal observed in his *Pensées,* "It is an astonishing thing that the mystery which is furthest removed from our knowledge—the mystery of the transmission of sin—is something without which we can have no knowledge of ourselves!"

MY PROFESSIONAL ADVENTURES IN PUBLIC LIFE

My father was the son of a farmer, and he wisely encouraged me in my youth to associate with coal miners and fisher folk in weekend ministry. Likewise, our church life revolved humbly around the nonconformist "gospel hall." So early on I learned that peasants tend to preserve living truths more faithfully than "city folk" because they live more simply. Indeed, in spending all my adult life in academia, I have grown profoundly dissatisfied with all forms of misplaced professionalism. Guilds for ethical standards for research, for competence in performances and for their accomplishments have their place. But to focus on professional endeavors alone blinds us to other ethical requirements. At each stage of my career, I have had to make hard choices consistent with my growing sense of disenchantment with the politics of professionalism.

After graduating from Edinburgh University, I entered the fledgling field of regional planning and was appointed geographer for the Clyde Valley Regional Planning Authority in 1944. The way our chief planner made arbitrary decisions based on politics rather than objective research led me to decide I would not invest my future in such a career, even though as a pioneer in the field I had great prospects. Later at Oxford, I was ready to resign my college fellowship on an issue of moral principle. Instead, after the issue was resolved, I was promoted to the position of college bursar. But I remained disenchanted with the "dreaming spires of Oxford." Still later when I served on the boards of Christian organizations, I found many of them more likely to act based on expediency rather than moral integrity.

When I was called to Vancouver to lead in the founding of Regent College, a respected Christian leader and family friend advised me, "Jim, whatever skills you develop in Christian leadership, make sure you become a good committee organizer and effective fundraiser." Instead, the first thing I did was decide that being a spiritual mentor directly conflicted with fundraising. To identify Christian leadership with finances is problematic. Certainly the pressures of institutional funding require tremendous spiritual resources, but sometimes I had to resist potential patronage and ask, "Are we spiritually ready to receive a million dollars?" Money deceptively promises ever-greater freedom, but at what cost to an institution's spiritual character? Do the board and administration become preoccupied with projects and development for their own sake so that the original vision is lost? Do politics supersede spiritual values? Do we feel as dependent on God for our continuance as when our institution was first founded?

In both church planting and college creation, I have experienced the progression from dynamic youthful fellowship to arthritic institutionalism. An institutional environment tends to become dominated by technical structures that leave little opportunity for the Spirit of God to influence decisions and guide direction. So institutional growth generates a life of its own—a bell curve of change from the personal to the bureaucratic. This curve used to occur slowly, perhaps over several centuries, but now it can occur in less than one generation. The intensification of

technology and the explosion of affluence have contributed greatly to
this switch from the personal to the institutional.

In this process, the personal call of God, which we experience, as
W. H. Auden put it, as "I would not, but alas, I must," becomes contrasted with the secular professional calling, that is, "I want to become
a certain kind of individual, so I will choose my own profession." The
institutional bell curve forms when the original call of God is overtaken
and suffocated by demands for professionalism and efficiency by way of
faculty handbooks, staff manuals, administrative assistants, and an insatiable budget. The original vision is eclipsed by money-making
projects. What may have begun as a simple community dedicated to
spiritual education and nurturing ends up an idolatrous environment of
professional careerism. The successful cloning between religious and
cultural values only intensifies the incredulity surrounding its avowed
"Christian" identity. As a friend of mine suggested, the church of Ephe-
sus probably lost its first love because its leaders were distracted from
sharing the good news of divine love by the study of apologetics and
theology. So we need to hold religious institutions lightly, knowing they
are but jars of clay. They may still contain the treasure of the gospel—if
somewhat precariously.

CHRISTIAN DISCIPLESHIP IS PERSONAL, NOT PROFESSIONAL

In the Gospels, Jesus' ministry is on a collision course with the vested
interests of the Jewish leaders and the temple economy in Jerusalem. His
example guides us in being *semper reformanda*. First, Jesus never used
power, for his kingdom is not of this world. Christian discipleship is not
a political reform movement, and coerced acts have no spiritual value.
We may need to relinquish our status and office if called on to define the
biblical values we live by. Resignation, submission to the powers that be
and abdication of political position may all be required. The Sermon on

the Mount is still the posture of Christian disciples today, and taking up the cross of Christ is the ultimate form of self-denial.

Second, Jesus was returning to the roots of Israel's early identity rather than creating a brand new revolutionary kingdom. Indeed, he was going back to God's original purpose for Israel, not Israel as later political consciousness would promote. Perhaps the current interest in the church's early fathers will likewise bring about another reformation of the church, rather than the ongoing conservative acceptance of our Reformation inheritance. We see now more critically that the Reformation itself was compromised from the beginning by geopolitical and cultural factors. As Dallas Willard has stated clearly in his book *Renovation of the Heart,* the impotence of institutions is that they cannot change the human heart. That is why Jesus did not send out his disciples to change governments or even to build churches, but to change hearts. His kingdom is not of this world. His revolution is not about social and political structures, but about changes of the mind and of the will and, indeed, of the heart. Here we might note how simple the house churches were to whom Paul addresses his letters. We note the lingua franca of *koine* Greek that is used. We concentrate on the simple focus given to the Lord's supper as the oath of allegiance. We read the instructions for a practical way of life intertwined with sound doctrine. It is worth noting that Jesus' parables are set within the simple peasant life and not in the political life of worldly religious leaders. As Matthew 21:45-46 puts it, "When the chief priests and the Pharisees heard Jesus' parables, they knew he was talking about them. They looked for a way to arrest him, but they were afraid of the crowd because the people held that he was a prophet."

Third, Jesus constantly attacks the conventional morality and hypocrisy of culture and politics. As discussed earlier, the disturbing demand of Christian discipleship is to have a unique relationship before God. We have already quoted Jesus' challenge: "If anyone comes to me and does not hate his father and mother, his wife and children, his brothers and sisters—yes, even his own life—he cannot be my disciple" (Lk 14:26). Matthew says the same thing more gently: "Anyone who loves his father or mother more than me is not worthy of me" (Mt 10:37). These verses imply that there are profound tensions between living conventionally and living specifically and uniquely as disciples of Christ. Clement of Alexandria interprets "hatred" as "not being diverted by irrational urges, nor allowing yourself to become dependent on conventional habits . . . in pleasing the world." In a unique relationship with Christ, there is both "hatred" and love, not as passions but as moral standards that separate evil from good. So a great love requires a great hate; the Messianic Servant is described as "hating iniquity and loving righteousness" (see Ps 45:7).

William Perkins, the early Puritan scholar, says the Christian has two callings: the primary one is to be a true disciple and child of God, and the secondary calling is a secular vocation, or even professional ministry. In fact, the Puritans first recognized with scholarly concern the seriousness of educational training required for pastoral ministry. But for them, this calling remained of secondary importance. The call to be children of God was the primary vocation, as it should be for us today. To make a career out of ecclesial ministry is essentially to become a "theological journalist." This person may accurately describe what others have thought and believed, but the reporter does not necessarily live out those truths. Such leaders are no better than the rulers of the temple, who eventually saw Jesus as their bitterest enemy. Their Christian ministry is no different than any other profession of secular life. I have appreciated the insight of British Prime Minister William E. Gladstone, who in his letters in the 1880s described his hesitation to advocate college fellowships in theology at Oxford and Cambridge, fearing that they might eventually secularize "the high calling of God."

Perhaps the essential issue lies in the difference between what

Kierkegaard called the "genius" and the "apostle." An apostle is an ordinary individual called by God to deliver a message to humanity—like someone who delivers mail. The genius, on the other hand, is someone with a natural gift who decides individually and ambitiously to pursue a chosen profession. The term "genius" refers not to exceptional intelligence but to those who are ingenious, or clever enough to use their wits to get what they want. As W. H. Auden notes, "Any genuine 'apostle' must say, 'I would not, but alas, I must.'" Such a "sent one" feels wholly inadequate to the task.

Not only are we called to witness to Christ's resurrection, but to experience existentially the call within our self. We state, like Paul, "When I am weak, then I am strong" (2 Cor 12:10). In this process we are "begraced," so that our natural instincts become subservient to transformative traits that actually change our personality. Indeed, we rely on death to self in order to act as divine messengers, not natural talents. No one volunteers for such a painful reversal, so that is why it is a calling and not a voluntary pursuit of individual interest and ambition. Perhaps it is this uncharted territory between being a clever self initiator and a weak apostle that generates so much of the surrealism of public ministry today. My friend, a former chief justice of a state federal court, was asked once by a law student what the first step was toward becoming a good judge. My friend's reply? "Having no ambition to be a judge!"

What Is Surrealism?

As the French artistic term *surrealisme* indicates, surrealism is "overrealistic," having a dreamlike atmosphere that expresses the subconscious mind. But this atmosphere only vaguely relates to ourselves and our intimate relationships. In a surrealistic world we cannot be fully awake to reality, for we do not have an adequate standard to know what reality is. It was in Tudor times that our Western consciousness first became aware of the surreal with the invention of Venetian glass mirrors. People could see their own face for the first time, no longer just a vague reflection on polished metal. With the use of the mirror, the self became much more self-conscious and therefore more expressible. Living in transition between the medieval and the modern worlds, the great dramatists began to promote a new seriousness for the pursuit of "sincerity" as expressive of this newly gained self-consciousness. At the same time it was challenged to expose the folly of dissimulation. Musically also, the harpsichord suitably expressed this simple definitive consciousness to be "sincere." The Puritans began to examine "cases of conscience" as the pursuit of moral sincerity. However, the more astute warned also about the innately self-deceptive nature of indwelling sin in the life of the Christian. Indeed, *Hamlet* is all about sincerity, as summed up in Polonius's paternal advice to Laertes:

> This above all: to thine own self be true,
> And it must follow, as the night the day,
> Thou canst not then be false to any man.

But sincerity is surreal if we forget we are self-deceptive by our nature as sinners. If "all the world's a stage, and all the men and women merely players," then role-acting is play-acting, because we all are fallen by nature. This change in self-consciousness to fantasize about sincerity is depicted in Shakespeare's visionary drama *A Midsummer Night's Dream*.

> And as imagination bodies forth
> The forms of things unknown, the poet's pen
> Turns them to shapes and gives to airy nothing
> A local habitation and a name.

But below the surface of imaginative frolics, fun and enchantment, there lurked violence, lust, jealousy, nightmares and even death. Shakespeare also depicts such surrealism in *The Tempest*, where

> We are such stuff
> As dreams are made on, and our little life
> Is rounded with a sleep.

Do these lines reflect the great dramatist's premonitions that the unexplored world ahead of "the modern" was to be feared, becoming more unreal the more humanized it became? Or is Shakespeare's *Tempest* merely anti-Faustian, leaving us with Ariel—not as "the lion of God" (the Hebrew meaning of *ariel*), but with a romantic, airy nothing that also fantasizes about the usurpation of God's realm?

The Psalter mirrors the soul's emotions very clearly, expressing forcibly in lament human incapacities as the manifestation of being sinners. But the remarkably successful pursuits of science and technology have increased the illusion of human independence from God, leading to the illusionary assumption that humanity creates its own reality. The contemporary icon of hyper-reality is the mass media of television. Hence surrealism is intensified by the many amplifications produced by technology, all expressive of new extensions of the human self. For the extreme form of surrealism is that we are self-contained and self-sufficient. Today, broader and vaster than a tsunami, surrealism appears to cover the whole planet, yet it is rarely exposed as false. Rather it is accepted uncritically as the best thing that ever happened to the human race. It deceptively persuades us that it is effective, powerful, tangible and indisputable.

SURREALISM AS A POSTMODERN "DIS-EASE"

Faustus isn't the only one who sold his soul to technology, for it now dominates our universal imagination. We need only to thumb through the old family photo album to see the vast changes technology has brought into our lives. "Personal identity" was once a social gift given to us by others; now it is a professional achievement we seek for ourselves by learning ever more techniques. "Home" was once a sacred space for Christian family life, but it has been taken over by gadgets. "Church" was once a community, but now it is a business enterprise uniting Christianity with capitalism and the entrepreneurial spirit. So when we uncritically accept further encroachments of technology without restraint, then surrealism has wholly taken over our lives. In this age of television and films, illusion dominates the human senses—far more than Shakespeare could have envisaged. Protests surrounding abortion, single-sex union and school prayer are feeble attempts to grasp some semblance of moral reality. But the campaigns have to be technologically proficient, for how else could the personal voice be heard today?

It is this supremacy of the technologically surreal to which organized Christianity has succumbed. Take, for example, the recent film *The Passion of the Christ*. People wept over its celluloid presentation as they never would have done in reading the Gospel narrative because it was so much more vivid to the senses. Was their response then hyper-real or real? Is the Sunday service more impressive when the PowerPoint presentation eclipses the preacher's sermon? Or does the message become more and more implausible with each technique used to market it? Does personal communication become muffled and withdrawn when the hearer is distracted by the medium?

These cultural trends affect our lives as Christians, most profoundly in our public roles of ministry, church membership and office, theological education and other institutional spheres. We are asleep morally in these areas, living contentedly in the surreal, yet we think we are serving God because we use up-to-date technical aids! Actually, it is in our public religious life that we are most culturally pressured by professionalism and pragmatism from without and distorted by neurotic drives from within.

Here we must radically question the nature of reality so that the boundaries between the real and the surreal do not become further blurred.

Most people would envy the success story of a religious institution. But success is a public and cultural rating, whereas faithfulness to God remains hidden and divinely evaluated. Moral failure occurs when original personal sacrifice is replaced by more worldly ambitions motivated by the reputation associated with a "successful" enterprise. Living faithfully to Christ is in contrast with success, for it is marked by the sacrificial reality of the cross of Christ. It is the height of surrealism to make a profitable career of the cross of Christ. As long as Christendom was part of the culture, its surrealism was not exposed, but today it is implausible to the world and so has become like it—too worldly. Even the world knows the difference between a sacrificial life and a self-centered one.

Further, institutions are often blind to sin because they are designed never to be wrong. The majority vote is always right. The bigger the institution, the less likely it is to be challenged. Indeed, statistical growth is seen as evidence that it is doing things right. Institutions are not set up to repent, nor to redress personal wrongs, nor to know themselves intimately. Rather they are designed to believe and trust in themselves politically rather than to believe and trust in God. They become idols rather than instruments for worshiping the living God. We can scarcely imagine how many idols we worship publicly if we are undiscerning and naïve about our public religious life.

Indeed, I'm not sure institutions can ever be truly called "Christian." Only a person can be a follower of Christ. As Paul Zahl, president of Trinity Episcopal School in Pittsburgh, states with the passion of his calling, "No one hears [the Word of God] collectively. It just doesn't happen. As a parish minister for thirty years, I have never met a person who actually hears collectively. . . . In short, we are not addressed collectively by the gospel." Indeed, John in his Gospel associates "the crowd" with that which is morally irresponsible, untruthful and false. Kierkegaard spoke of "the single individual" as one who has faith in God alone, standing always in God's presence. God defines that one, and before him one alone has reality. Then one knows one is a sinner, yes, but that one is extraordinary, too, because of the grace of God.

Traditionally, *reality* has referred to the things around and within us that we cannot alter (the word comes from the Latin *res*, which means a "thing" we can identify). Instead, argues Albert Borgmann, we have created a substitute, disposable reality that we can adopt and dispense with at our whim. It is created by our own psychic needs in interplay with material culture. In the disposable reality of consumerism, recorded music, shopping malls and theme parks predominate and shut out more humane environments. Today, disposable reality eclipses commanding realities that would challenge us as moral agents.

True reality is multidimensional, characterized by depth and variety. False reality, or surrealism, is determined by the pragmatic, technical and impersonal. In accepting it we become surreal ourselves, abdicating our personal awareness in exchange for a dreamlike and selective quality of perception. Since we all do this regularly, seeing ourselves as others see us helps us test the validity of our perceptions. A scientist interprets reality as a realm of problems that require solutions. A philosopher seeks reality in the clarification of puzzles in the communication of "truth." A religious person focuses on the mysteries of life, either liturgically or theologically. A businessperson sees reality in projects, programs, consumption and organizations. So a realistic Christian faith needs to incorporate all these dimensions of reality at a personal level and yet not be seduced and mastered by any one of them.

REALITY AS A PERSONAL NARRATIVE

We begin with our own perceptions. Perhaps I am more critical of the institutional church because I have always been a "freechurchman," persuaded of the merit of congregational ecclesiology. I grew up in the Brethren, where "the priesthood of all believers" was a central focus. Nor did I ever believe in infant baptism; it seemed to me a myth of institutional religion. I spent twenty-five formative years at Oxford, where it was acceptable to be religious as long as you were Anglican. But to be associated with the Brethren was to be considered oddly sectarian. This affected my intellectual identity, to say the least.

I also grew up in Scottish, not English, church life, with cultural differences inherited from the Reformation. The English civil war of the seventeenth century further promoted party differences—Whig or Tory, blue collar or white collar, grammar school or public school, congregational or state churchmanship. Growing up, children were on the outside or the inside of many English clubs, each with their magic inner circles like nesting Russian dolls. These experiences made a person either marginal or centrist. Naturally, when you live on the outside you can be more creatively critical of "the shining ones in the Dorchester hotel," as the poet John Betjeman puts it. Perceptions are always affected, if not controlled, by previously acquired conceptions and experiences.

It was Richard Baxter, suffering with his fellow Christians in the English civil war, who opted out of being a "party man" to call himself a "mere Christian." C. S. Lewis, an Irishman in Oxford, developed a similar distaste for denominationalism, calling himself "a man of the foothills, neither very high nor very low" who also advocated *Mere Christianity.* I myself was not considered quite sound by some of the "Evangelical party" because I urged evangelicals to invite Lewis to speak at their public meetings; he was never invited. Moreover, I lived for seven years with Nicholas Zernov, then leader of Eastern Orthodoxy in Britain and a friend of monks from Athos. Nicholas was given the nickname "Exhibit A," and I was "Exhibit B." The faculty at Regent College today owes at

least some of its distinctive transdenominational character to this back-
ground. A mere Christian I am still content to be.

This then is an issue we all have to ask: how much ecclesial surrealism
have we inherited from the histories of our denominations and our own
narratives within them? The religious life has accumulated great layers
of superstition and mythology. The emphasis on religious buildings,
priestly vestments, liturgy and the ceremonial traditions surrounding the
Eucharist and the seasonal feasts of the religious calendar can all
threaten to turn Christ into a myth.

How surreal is our church life? In answering this question we must
go back to the Peace of Westphalia in 1648, as my friend Bruce Hindmarsh has written about. This event ended thirty years of savage religious wars on the continent of Europe. It shattered the concept of
"Christendom," leaving us divided ever since. Perhaps we go further
back, to the origins of Christendom. We are told that it commenced with
Constantine's establishment of Christianity as the state religion of the Roman empire in A.D. 325. Reversing his predecessors' policy of decentral-
ization of governance, Constantine decided Christianity would be the
ideal choice for his political objectives. After all, a universal god was perfect for a universal empire! Constantine was forty years old when he
"converted" from being a ruthless pagan, and the true nature of his
Christianity has always been debatable. His legacy has been the shadow
of Caesarism inherited by the Roman papacy, as later czarism took over
in the Eastern church. Ecclesiology has been confused ever since.

√   The lesson from the church's witnesses is that only the risen Christ can
provide Christians with a sense of personal reality throughout all the confused history of the church. Perhaps, then, the end of Christendom high-
lights the reality of this living Christ. As Malcolm Muggeridge stated,
"Christ himself abolished Christendom before it began by stating that his
kingdom was not of this world. . . . Christendom began with the Emperor

Constantine. Christianity began with the Incarnation." The latter alone offers hope for the future of Christianity. Yet the contemporaneous character of Christ is balanced and sustained by the historicity of Christ. Christ lived, died and rose again in Palestine under the reign of Pontius Pilate. The events of his life actually happened then, just as he can actually be present with us now. He is not a "universal idea," some Gnostic principle. Becoming a follower of Christ implies that it is specifically Christ we follow, and no one else. He makes us real as no one else can.

Muggeridge often mentioned to me how impressed he was by a distinction of William Blake's. When we look with the eye, we project on the outside world all our internal fantasies and desires—indeed, all our preconceptions and misconceptions. But Christ looks through us, knowing our inmost thoughts. So with Christ within us, we are able to look through the eye to see all that is culturally distorted. A late convert to Christian faith, Muggeridge concluded, "The reality of Christ is Christ. The reality of Christ lies in the fact that through him the distinction between fantasy and reality becomes clear. . . . Fantasy comes from seeing with the eye, from reflecting in your eye what is outside. Reality can only be seen by looking through the eye. With Christ we look through rather than with."

Speaking of the end of Christendom does not mean we deny its earthly glory, as if we could after witnessing the galleries of Rome or Florence. Its art, sculpture, music and literature are the fabric of Western civilization. But today we are surrounded by the bureaucratic rather than the baroque; it is our contemporary form of surrealism. Bureaucracy has greatly expanded since World War II with the phenomenal expansion of parachurch organizations—capitalism gone religious. McDonald's has become the prototype for religious consumerism: we sell new programs in our megachurches, seek franchises worldwide and cite limitless numbers to prove our success.

KIERKEGAARD'S CRITIQUE OF CHRISTENDOM

Late in his life (1855) Kierkegaard wrote his *Attack on Christendom*, which helps us see through ecclesial unreality. Indeed, in all his writings Kierkegaard sought out reality. He believed that most people took refuge from honesty by sheltering in a life of habit, of rote Christianity. Growing up on the heathland of Jutland, he envisioned his lonely life as a solitary fir tree standing vertically against the flatness of the cultural landscape. Instead of the ten commandments of biblical faith, the bourgeois Danish culture lived under "the law of Jante," which decreed, "You shall not be different from anyone else." No one has indicted institutionalized religion more deeply than Kierkegaard, before or since. In his *Journals*, we note that he began to ask how one becomes a real Christian in a pseudo-Christian order. Was it necessary for him to leave the security of the established order "to trust himself with absolute confidence in God over a depth of seventy thousand fathoms"?

Theory never can understand more than our life expresses. Kierkegaard saw that the Hegelian Bishop Mynster, the primate of the Danish church, could only "preach Christianity fast aground in a delusion." The result was that "in an impermissible and unlawful way people have become, knowing about Christ, when the only permissible way is to be believing" Christ. Knowing about Christ allows the natural mind to operate without grace, merely as a student. Thus in Christendom Kierkegaard saw the natural man free to act as he wanted, with the world and the church never separated and everyone claiming to live in a "Christian country."

Kierkegaard recognized also that two millennia of church history distances the believer from the gospel. But Christ is "the absolute contemporary," so two thousand years makes no difference to his daily presence within us. Provided we remain conscious of sin and the power of grace,

we experience the true reality of being always with him. Merely admiring √
Jesus maintains a false distance, but our personal obedience in walking
daily with him implies immediacy. It makes faith so vivid that we suffer
for it. Therefore we will give offense by carrying the cross (Mt 15:1-12).
The offense has to do with the uniqueness of Christ, so we embrace him
in our lowliness. Anyone who depicts reality must be of humble character, prepared to suffer greatly in renouncing the ways of the world. But
we only live once, so a life well lived in Christ is already related rightly
with eternity.

Christian earnestness is the antidote Kierkegaard would prescribe for √
our Christendom-like institutional surrealism. He develops this idea in
The Concept of Anxiety, associating Christian earnestness with self-under-   —
standing before God. Indeed, becoming real is only possible when we √
humbly face the sin in our own life and then live in the light of the eternal. Without a true awareness of sin and of grace, our life is condemned   ✳
to unreality. Moreover, all the elements of our personality must be involved so that faith deals with our emotions, cognition and connation,
as well as things spiritual, all integrated in our personal living out of the
gospel. Then the unity of the temporal and the eternal within our own
unique person introduces a new state of being.

Today, people are often referring to the sociology of religion when they
speak about "the end of Christendom." The demise is obvious statistically
and socially, especially in Western Europe. But social explanations, even
by Christian writers, may explain without exploring deeply what we need
to reform. That is why Kierkegaard is still required reading.

SELF-FOCUSED CREATIVITY IS NEVER INNOCENT

I have been trying to process such reflections for more than fifty years,
since I first heard a public lecture on Kierkegaard at Oxford's Ashmolean
Museum in 1959. But in the midseventies I also began to read the novels

of William Golding, recipient of the Nobel Prize in 1983. Fascinated by the lurking reality of evil in all human efforts, he once told an interviewer, "Man is a fallen being . . . gripped by original sin: a creature who produces evil as a bee produces honey." Golding lived with many tensions. One was his father, who as a science teacher "was incarnate omniscience." He wanted his son to climb up the scientific ladder, "rung after factual rung, with Sir James Jeans and Professor Einstein . . . waiting at the top to sign me on." But instead of achieving this clear scientific view from the top, young Bill climbed the branches of the tree in the garden, hiding in its vestigial depths, listening to lovers in the lane below and delving into the mysteries of human beings. Later, as a naval lieutenant, he experienced the senseless violence of war, which convinced him that confidence placed in scientific humanism was absurd. He interpreted a lack of moral vision as the loss of imagination and of the awareness of the evil potency of the will. Golding also argued that when we ignore the crucial tension between analysis and mystery—as "felt by the pulses" of being fully alive—then our own creativity will deceive us most of all.

Most schoolchildren have read *Lord of the Flies*. As a moral fable, it frightens many children from reading further. In the novel, all teenagers suffer from "the terrible disease of being human," discovering that their most dangerous enemy lurks inside themselves. It is Cain killing his brother all over again in murderous jealousy. Since then, René Girard has pointed out that envy is actually the origin of human culture. Significantly, it is Cain and his descendants who built a city and became progressively inventive and creative (Gen 4:17-24). In one of his last novels, *The Spire* (1966), Golding explores this theme further: what happens when human enterprise builds "for the glory of God" without the need of the Holy Spirit?

Living in Salisbury, Golding could see St. Mary's Cathedral from his window as he wrote his novel. It is the tallest church spire in England, towering above the rooftops of the old town. Yet the character Jocelin, the medieval dean of the cathedral, decides that one spire is not enough; he needs another as well. This second tower dominates the plot of the novel. The master of works, Roger Mason, knows that the badly chosen site is on a swamp, as often happened in the Middle Ages. It was fortunate the cathedral had not already collapsed. But two spires! "Don't do it," Mason cautions. "It is crazy to try!"

But the dean's actions are all about self-worship, not God: "I thought I was chosen; a spiritual man, loving above all; and given specific work to do. And from this followed the debts, the deserted church, the discord. Much, much more. More than you can ever know. Because I really do not know myself. Reservations, connivances. The work before everything." What was originally purported to be for the glory of God to enhance the house of worship becomes a ruined, empty place, creating gossip, backbiting and scandals, even destroying lives. The irony is that the tower did not fall, but as in the story of Babel, everything else collapsed. As he lay dying, Jocelin mourned, "I thought I was doing a great work; and all I was doing was bringing ruin and breeding hate."

I read *The Spire* in 1978 during the height of a power struggle in a Christian institution, and it radically changed my perception of Christian ministry. None of us can do the work of the Lord in isolation and with false motives, let alone merely for self-preservation. The words of David kept pulsating through me with every breath I took: "Create in me a pure heart, O God, and renew a steadfast spirit within me. Do not . . . take your holy Spirit from me" (Ps 51:10-11). Only with a pure heart can we see reality. However deeply you or I feel injustice, having God's Spirit is far more precious than self-vindication, which is fantasy, not reality. I did not want to follow the way of Jocelin, crying out, "If David could not build the temple because there was blood on his hands, what is to be said of us, and of me?" You have probably known "Christian leaders" who have stabbed others in the back to keep on top. What is prayer if it degenerates into mere self-will deluded into thinking it is all for God's glory?

At the end of his tragic life, the dean despairs. "What is faith?" he asks Father Adam, who is trying to comfort him. "Would you like to see my faith? It lies there in the old chest. A little log book in the left hand corner." The tower represents the dean's faith in himself, which causes his uncertain faith in God to crash in ruins. The tower, once seen as an act of devotion, is now a monument to a willful life and a lustful heart. Its projection expresses his selfish neurotic drives. Digging the foundations of the tower is entering the cellar of his own sinful life. At first, his lack of prayer stems from pride until he can no longer pray at all. Then in his delusion of being a servant of God, he escapes into a dream world, "uncountry," he calls it, which has "consent, and no sin." Now everyone talks of his project as "Jocelin's Folly" (as in the French *folie*, meaning "delight" or "favorite abode")—literally, "the abode of his own pride."

Ever since I read *The Spire*, I have been fearful of building towers, for they usually become mausoleums for our own dry bones. Cremation is better, scattering the ashes of a selfless ministry into a thousand hearts. Then only the risen Lord can make "these bones live," as Ezekiel saw in his vision (Ezek 37:3).

But the world cannot understand such surrealism. It would see Jocelin as a heroic figure of Greek tragedy, perhaps a scapegoat for other people's faults. For, says Aristotle, the action of a tragedy centers on an error of judgment, a false step, cause and effect, being in the wrong place at the wrong time. The Greek word for tragedy (*harmatia*) does not imply a moral wrong or fault. So when we live emotionally as tragic heroes, we live with surrealism. Saul Bellow, another novelist of moral fable, has indicted this contemporary "romantic despair." It is, he says, "naggingly conscious of the absurd . . . absurdly portentous, not metaphysically 'absurd.'" By this Bellow means that being "romantic" and "heroic" are both unreal and therefore humanly "absurd," whereas the metaphysically "absurd" is how the world may view the religious life.

The question then is, before whom are our lives justified: ourselves, others or God? Pride goes before a fall, and being aware of this fact is Christian realism. Jocelin is proud and prayerless. Too late he discovers his lack of self-knowledge and the reality that "there is no innocent work." Whenever self-obsession replaces the reality of God, we are set up for a spectacular fall—or Fall, as in the Garden. Christian service is too big to embrace in my arms as "my ministry." In rereading *The Spire*, which I have done several times, I never cease to be grateful for its terrifying depiction of how sin crouches at the door—as Cain learned—of our most idealistic schemes. They will ensnare us if we hold them too willfully. To identify the work of God with our own narcissistic dreams √ is to court ultimate disillusionment.

There is no doubt that technology has brought forth the most complex and imposing creations in human history. The ingenuity, coordination and devotion apparent in technological advances are epochal, so the necessary reforms must also be radical and personally costly. They have to be undertaken intelligently, concretely, voluntarily and with great vision. What can motivate and empower us more than the cross of Christ, the God-Man who "became poor, so that you through his poverty might become rich" (2 Cor 8:9)? Nothing is more tragic than Christian minis- √ tries and institutions that lose their Christian focus, becoming secular in spirit and motive, all in the name of Christ! It surely is apostasy when the bureaucracy of the church becomes a stumbling block to the gospel!

FOUR

The Journey
Toward Becoming a Person

You have led me from my bondage and set me free by all those roads,
by all those loving means, that lay within your power and charity.

DANTE
Paradiso

For we are what he has made us,
created in Christ Jesus for good works,
which God prepared beforehand to be our way of life.

EPHESIANS 2:10 NRSV

Rather than lamenting the forces of secularization overtaking our society, perhaps we should reflect on the loss of the plausibility of the Christian faith to our society. The sociologist Bryan Wilson defines secularization as "the process whereby religious thinking, practices, and institutions lose social significance." This statement implies that desecularization can occur if Christianity regains social significance. In a postmodern society, where the self-making of one's own identity prevails, providing selfless love, compassionate concern and a joyful moral serenity can become a medium for the gospel.

We need much more than lucidity to cut through the surreal. Certainly we must use light and truth to penetrate the fog. But we also need tranquility, safety, certainty and enjoyment in the gospel. Our faces need to shine with the joy of the Lord. Christian joy, as I have been privileged to experience, shines serene as a star, as Christ's own peace. Joyous serenity appears and re-appears like the face of an angel looking through a window we cannot open, beckoning us to look beyond our own little world. This joy is evident in Giovanni Bellini's painting *The Agony in the Garden* in the National Gallery in London; it is the radiant emblem of divine grace in a darkened world.

As we have seen, the Christian life is dialectical. To affirm "It is this, but it is also that" helps us avoid making absolutes out of creaturely things. The opposite attitude, which comes down to "this-is-all-there-is-ism," reflects an idolization of ideologies from which the postmodern culture is now in revolt. But because of sin, we also need an inverse dialectic between our natural man and our spiritual man (see appendix). There is continuity between these two states yet also profound discontinuity, similarity yet sharp contrast. The process of the inverse dialectic involves negation; sin must be restrained, indeed denied as having no place in God's scheme of things. As we shall see, the pilgrimage motif found in Dante and Bunyan has helped me discern this inverse dialectic; their works demonstrate how misrelated we are to God because of our nature as sinful rebels. Our natural, isolated individualism contrasts strongly with God's intent to redeem us communally to become persons in Christ.

IN PURSUIT OF THE PERSONAL

I have long thought that failure to sustain the personal is the worst feature of modern life. Indeed, is this not at the heart of the cultural crisis of our times? All efforts to create community fail if we try to engender community as self-centered individuals. It should be a primary Christian concern to express our faith personally in growing awareness of our new identity as persons in Christ. Years ago, when Mary Rockefeller was president of the YWCA, she told me quietly that she was committed "to bringing the 'C' back into the organization." In that same spirit, can we not focus more on the "C" in our own commitment to becoming PICs—persons in Christ?

Ideally, the focal point of the personal is family life. But for many of us it's not that straightforward. The ways we are treated privately at home as children become the ways we treat others publicly later in life, and there can be significant gaps in the personal during both phases. But our public education can be a happy intervention. For me this started with the classical, or *paideia*, education I received at Oxford. Lectures were less important than the tutorial system, and priority was given to the student, not to the subject matter per se. Alan Bullock, head of one of the colleges I taught in, once assured me that it was an immature teacher who saw the subject as all-important. Rather, a mark of academic maturity is to value the personal formation of the student in the light of the discipline being taught. It was inspiring to witness the selflessness of a few tutors who forfeited their own publishing ambitions for the sake of giving their best to their students. This has persuaded me ever since to cultivate a compassionate, not just critical, scholarship. This does not imply disciplinary carelessness in the academic discipline, but recognizing teaching as a means to a higher end: the education of other persons.

Listening to literally thousands of students over sixty years of mentoring, I have been enriched by their shared experiences of personal life. They have taught me that we should welcome those knocks at the office door not as interruptions, but as fresh opportunities to learn more from human life and its diverse relationships and experiences. We live much more extensively than what we experience within our own egos. Personal tragedies only reinforce this. I shall mourn all my life for two young people who committed suicide, and also for the suicide of a lonely philosophy don, Michael Foster. I thought I knew them all well, but alas, not well enough. Since then, I have learned to take the relational wounds of confidantes with compassionate seriousness. We can never give enough understanding, recognition, kindness, empathy and encouragement to others. Uniqueness is a great gift of God, but a great curse without God. And who can understand the uniqueness of the other without God's loving presence within?

In the past two decades it has become popular to recognize the theological importance of the doctrine of the Trinity in the analogy of "persons," human and divine. Being relational is thus given a theological foundation for human anthropology. But I have learned to be suspicious of popularity in academia. It can produce wrong motives even for right choices. When certain scholars write enthusiastically about becoming persons in Christ and then divorce their spouses, I wonder if even trinitarian theology has become just another scholarly topic. It has become popular to apply the Greek term *perichoresis* to the triune God, to the divine mutual indwelling of each one in the other, and then apply the same concept to the Christian life, our indwelling in Christ as the Holy Spirit indwells us. But John of Damascus cautioned that *perichoresis* was a human term applied by some of the early church fathers to the Trinity. So now we must remind ourselves that to speak of "persons, human and divine" is not to assume that humans are analogous to the Godhead. Always there is the Otherness of God. He is holy, wholly Other, and Karl Barth warned against speaking of the divine Persons as if they were similar to human persons. John Zizoulas has suggested, perhaps unconvincingly to Western Christians, that "persons" is an ecclesial connotation bestowed by the church on church members only through the rite of baptism. Perhaps, too, he has attributed to Gregory of Nyssa a view of the idea of the "person" that is more contemporary than patristic. It is

misguided to assume that our contemporary sense of consciousness was
the same in the past. Human consciousness does not remain the same,
but changes through time, as our environment also changes.

I gave my heart to the Lord as a small child and was baptized by my
own choice at twelve years old, but it wasn't until my twenties that I deliberately chose to find my identity completely in Christ. It was then that
2 Timothy 1:12 became so meaningful for me: "I am not ashamed, for I
know the one in whom I have put my trust, and I am sure that he is able
to guard until that day what I have entrusted to him" (NRSV). Previously,
I assumed that verse meant I had entrusted my soul to Christ in the event
of my death. Now I reinterpreted it to mean that I committed my day-
to-day identity to him. I could then experience the profound joy and
peace that comes with being found in Christ, as Paul states (Phil 3:8-9).

As a culture we tend more than ever to hold our identity in our own
hands, and because of this we also sense more acutely the fragility of
such a precarious identity. Perhaps this is why we have become so narcissistic and driven to self-serving professional accomplishment. In contrast, the apostle Paul interprets even his religious ambitions as dross
compared with the incomparable pursuit of knowing Christ and being
found in him, "not having a righteousness of [his] own." I find that many
young Christians today are receiving a double message: It's great that
they are a Christian, but their professional identity matters much more.
No! A genuine Christian existence means we are so taken over by Christ
that we have a whole new identity defined by our encounter with him.
Because of this, Paul's statement in Galatians 2:20 has been a pivotal text
for me: "I no longer live, but Christ lives in me." My self still lives and,
alas, often gets in the way of Christ in me, but a new porosity of the self
is taking place, often painfully and slowly, yet definitively. The conviction is growing that if anything is done for God in my life, it is not I who
do it but the indwelling Spirit of Christ.

In the late 1960s, I was asked to contribute to a series of essays titled *Why I Am Still a Christian,* which was a response to Bertram Russell's book *Why I Am Not a Christian.* As scholars we were asked to write about how we integrated our faith with our professional discipline. My essay was titled "A God-Centered Personality," with little reference to my profession since I wanted to emphasize the central importance of being a person in Christ. I saw then, and still do, that "the reality and the relevance of the Christian faith is its power of the personal, its insight and truth concerning personal relations and purpose."

THE CHALLENGE OF PERSONALIST PHILOSOPHERS

If you are tempted to think my appeal here is only devotional and therefore "soft," I respond with the assertion that living out as a person takes hard thinking indeed! Michael Polanyi was one of my early neighbors at Oxford, so I read his work *Personal Knowledge* as soon as it was published in 1959. Although he might have received the Nobel Prize had he remained as a research chemist, he chose to become a philosopher of science to combat current false Marxist interpretations. It was a selfless act in defense of the truth, recognizing that scientists are fully and personally involved with their subject matter, regardless of ideology. For there is no impersonal scientific knowledge.

At about the same time, John Macmurray, a Scottish philosopher at my alma mater, Edinburgh University, was also reflecting on the personal. He proposed that the locus of the person was not thought, as Descartes had postulated, but action. As persons we are what we are only in active relation to other persons. So our attention should not be on the identity of the thinking individual, but on the active matrix within which individuality takes shape. The self should not theoretically be conceived of as a subject, but more intentionally evaluated as an agent. "The isolated purely individual self is a fiction," Macmurray declared.

Certainly this point of view is closer to the Fourth Gospel's claim that from eternity the Father and the Son have coinhered by the action of the Holy Spirit. As Jesus states in Matthew 11:27, "All things have been committed to me by my Father. No one knows the Son except the Father, and no one knows the Father except the Son and those to whom the Son chooses to reveal him." While Macmurray grew up in a pious Christian Brethren home, he became disillusioned with the abstract ways he experienced religious dogma. He wanted to live according to the following maxim: "All meaningful knowledge is for the sake of action, and all meaningful action is for the sake of friendship." His writings later influenced British Prime Minister Tony Blair to reinterpret socialism as needing to become less ideological and more personal. The Gifford Lectures by Macmurray were published in 1957 as *The Form of the Personal* in two volumes: *The Self as Agent* and *Persons in Relation*. These have been constant reading for me ever since.

Polanyi and Macmurray's philosophies had their seeds in the beginning of the early nineteenth century with Georg Hamann in Germany, a friend of Immanuel Kant's, then with Søren Kierkegaard, who much admired Hamann. From them followed a number of personalist philosophers from the 1920s onward, including Martin Buber, Emmanuel Mounier and Karl Brunner. Each added new perspectives on the personal, and each was reacting to the depersonalization of modern culture as brought about by the two world wars, the Holocaust, the growth of scientific abstraction and the challenge of Marxism. Indeed, for a time Macmurray was attracted to Marxism, as were other idealists in the 1930s.

More recently, Emmanuel Levinas has proposed that ethics is a sense of infinite responsibility to "the other" (French *l'autrui*), indeed that interhuman relationships have ultimate primacy. This outlook is now producing new perspectives in the social sciences. As a result, the contrast between individualism as pathological and relational personhood as health-giving is being more widely acknowledged. A prisoner of the Russian gulag, Levinas attributed his survival to the conviction that he was living for the sake of his wife, not for himself. Life for the other became the basis of his ethics. He also concluded that cognitive exercise could not explain the process of face-to-face interaction with another person. Relationships simply cannot be described with language and thought.

Broadly speaking, all these thinkers denied the rationalist universe of the Enlightenment. They rejected its three basic assumptions: that all genuine questions can be answered, otherwise there is something wrong with the question; that all issues of human life are knowable; and that all forms of knowledge are compatible with each other. All these thinkers therefore critiqued intellectualism.

TECHNOLOGICAL SOCIETY IN AN IMPERSONAL UNIVERSE

Intellectualism, however, is a product as well as a cause of technology. Max Weber early on recognized that a society dominated by science, technology and bureaucracy contributes profoundly to "the disenchantment of the world." This not only comes about through the disappearance of a sense of mystery, but also through the loss of the personal dimension in human life. Erich Kahler argued that technology produces "cold consciousness" through detachment and depersonalization while intensifying an artificial, pseudo-emotional sensibility. Desensitized, we are deadened to the plight of others, content to urge political action or even support charitable organizations, but never getting involved on a personal level. The media filter our moral values for us, so that in the decline of moral consciousness we also feel powerless, meaningless and even puerile. Our inner and our outer selves become distended, leading to fragmentation, alienation, nonrecognition, inattention and loneliness.

The psychiatrist J. H. van den Berg has argued that addressing loneliness is at the core of the field of psychiatry. Loneliness is the result of ambiguous

relationships, which in a technological society are bred by the double threat
of meaninglessness and powerlessness. For the pursuit of power, which is
the goal of technology, cannot provide meaningful relations, but the omni-
presence of technology produces only an illusion of power. As this illusion
of power grows, legitimacy and shared meaning degenerate into superfici-
ality. The conflict between power and meaning, along with the resulting
loneliness and alienation, leads to other cultural disorders as well: fear, violence and the loss of selfhood. The disease of sociosis breeds neurosis—
that is, social ills become individual ills. So we are all part of "the lonely
crowd," as David Riesman described our technological society. The blur-
ring between the neurotic and the normal continues to weaken personal
values and our ability to sustain reliable relationships.

As we saw in the previous chapter, the corporate and individual lives
of Christians unfortunately show little or no difference from the rest of
industrialized society. Technology penetrates our church life so that even
church members experience intense loneliness. Alienation may seem inevitable in a secular world, but it also decreases the credibility of church
life. Hence the growing reaction of many Christians: "I don't go to
church any longer, for I want to be real about my faith and how I cultivate relationships."

Ironically, in the business world major efforts are being made to
change the impersonal nature of organizational culture into one that is
organic, personal and intelligent. Business has become more custom-
ized, service is more personal, and more flexible organizations allow in-
itiatives to rise from the lower ranks of employees. The absence of traits
such as compassion, empathy and emotional intelligence is condemned
as "institutional toxicity." For a poisonous atmosphere of envy, competi-
tion, fear, distrust and loneliness cannot make full use of the work force.
But this attempt at better relations remains a pragmatic solution that is
incapable of dealing with the most fundamental human issues.

One expert in organizational behavior realized this when he was diagnosed with dangerous melanoma. Suddenly, he appreciated the world of compassion and empathy. As he compared the way his nurses treated him to his business environment, he began to see what was wrong. He noted also that when passengers on the doomed flights of September 11, 2001, were being held hostage by terrorists, they did not use their cell phones to call about business matters; they simply said, "I love you" to their loved ones. When facing death, nothing else matters. So the irony is that organizational experts are advocating more personalized relationships because it's pragmatic to do so, but organized religion lags behind because its leaders do not have the same profit-driven incentive!

Yet despite these efforts in the professional world, an insufficient personal life is the affliction of most people today. We are paying a huge price to succeed in the "I-it" world of science and technology. We needn't pay this price—we can do a great deal to counteract sociosis if we make persons matter more than things or even institutions. My wife and I are privileged to witness this in the careers of all our children. Their personal qualities effectively bring blessings to others and to themselves. But the great barrier to living with a conviction of the supremacy of the personal is that our professional identity often remains more important than our friendships. A career tends to have priority over character. Family life takes a heavy toll when a whole society believes professionalism reigns supreme and both husband and wife think they must be on career tracks to have a meaningful life.

Another negative feature of technology is its dispersive nature. It makes us feel homeless and unfocused. These ideas are connected, for the word "focus" (Latin *fogur*) refers to the hearth, the traditional center of the household. In Roman society, the union of a marriage was sanctified at the hearth, and in other times the dead were buried under the hearth. The fireside has traditionally been the place for the family to gather in work and in leisure. In turn, home was the focus of security, significance, shelter and celebration. It assigned to each family member his or her tasks for the day, forming a web of nurturing human relationships. Later, the center of medieval life was the cathedral, and within the cathedral the high altar—a spiritual hearth—was the central focus, as indeed the Eucharist was the focus of Christian faith. Clearly, then, a life of focus implies evaluation, choice and integration of personal values into daily life so that they become habits of the character.

All this is missing in the technical world. Indeed, without focus we are generating a runaway technology. The mobility induced by technology has conquered space in remarkable ways, so we jet around the world and enjoy unparalleled opportunities for discourse through the use of mobile phones and e-mail. But our families have been disrupted; home life and small communities have suffered. Today, our home increasingly reflects the wealth we acquire beyond its boundaries. And our heat no longer comes from the hearth but from a large generating plant that fuels a whole city.

Technology also removes a sense of scale and proportion from human relationships. Vividly I remember a rally in Dallas in 1972 when a well-known Christian leader shouted, "I love you all!" through the microphone to thousands of impressionable young people. "You are a liar!" I found myself muttering. "How can you say that and really mean it?" We are enjoined to love our neighbor as our self, but our neighbor is determined by the scale of space and time to which we are personally limited. Only God can infinitely love the world. Techniques do extend our powers, but they also tend to create surrealistic, mirage-like effects, as noted previously.

At a deeper level, technology also suffocates the human identity because it is evolutionary rather than historical. This is partly the result of progressive scientific discoveries, which lead proponents of Marxism and its variants to assume that people will evolve further by new techniques as they are developed. This "organic" model lacks historical, and therefore personal, consciousness. It perhaps explains why people, in reaction, have discovered a renewed passion to express their own narrative—they don't want to be lost in the impersonal evolutionary crowd.

GOD AS THE SOURCE OF PERSONHOOD

Because loneliness is a key element of our technological society, we need to remember that a central element of the Christian faith is a deep relationship with God. Even when our relations with other people are ambiguous, we can still enter into a clearly defined relationship with the triune God of grace. If we accept Levinas's basic understanding of ethics as being lived in the presence of the other person, then we can no longer accept the Cartesian tenet of "I think, therefore I am." Rather we say to God, "Here I am; relate to me." This is closer to the experience of the young Samuel, and indeed all the Old Testament prophets, as well as Saul of Tarsus on the way to Damascus. For as we have seen, human life cannot be reduced to comprehension; it requires personal encounter and relations to grow.

When I was at Oxford, Leonard Hodgson was Regius Professor of Theology and also a personal colleague. I read his pioneering book on the Trinity years before the contemporary interest in the Trinity began. Colin Gunton was a student at Hertford College while I was teaching there, and he has been as influential as any contemporary theologian in contributing to this renewed interest in trinitarian theology; he, too, has influenced me.

Another contemporary influence for me has been a book by Greek theologian John Zizioulas titled *Being as Communion*. Zizioulas radically sees "the person" as essentially a theological entity reflective of the triune God who in grace shares his likeness with us. Each unique person of the

Trinity—including humans, according to Zizioulas—realizes himself through and in the others in a reality of communion and community. This affirms Paul's prayer: "For this reason I kneel before the Father, from whom his whole family in heaven and on earth derives its name . . . that Christ may dwell in your hearts through faith . . . being rooted and established in love" (Eph 3:14-17). Sublime as this prayer is, the study of theology can be abstract, even when it touches on personal relationships, so it is possible to be a theological expert and still practice poor relations with others. Perhaps it is because the motivations of such study often remain shallowly critical rather than pastoral in intent.

A lack of passion is another trait of technological society. Passion enables us to leap beyond ourselves, indeed beyond our calculated transactions of counting money, rationalizing, and thus remaining within the finite. Instead of passion for the beyond, we often substitute envy of our rivals, of those possessing what we desire. Often this spirit is mimetic, coming not just from within ourselves but from imitation of each other. It is prompted by a passive acquiescence to emotion, a primitive state that indicates a lack of self-determination. It is reflected in much of the popular music in contemporary culture, which immerses the self in inarticulate moods. When the will is freed to be articulate and self-determining, then a more creative, less passive state becomes apparent, one that is willing to seek adventure and take risks. Aesthetic passion is a higher level still, moving beyond physical passion toward a sense of beauty, a realm beyond oneself. Moral passion moves higher still in empathy toward the other and an earnest desire to relate in community.

But joyous Christian passion is the highest level of all. It involves an identity outside of ourself; as George Herbert expressed it, it is being a "soul in pilgrimage" in prayerful communion with God. Such redemptive passion signals an intimate relationship with God, a hungering and thirsting after him. The consequence of such loving passion for God is a kind of suffering as we seek the infinite within a finite frame. Thus Christian passion is not momentary ecstasy. It does not fly from unhappiness. Nor is it merely sensual, nor does it find satisfaction in the here and now. Rather Christian passion elevates the soul, lifting it beyond the allurements of the world to become personally engaged in what the Puritans called "heavenly-mindedness." Richard Baxter describes it as "the saints' everlasting rest," and C. S. Lewis in his space fiction calls it the experience of "Perelandra."

DANTE AS OUR GUIDE ON THE JOURNEY INTO PERSONHOOD

Such Christian passion views life in wide landscapes, such as the one Tolkien outlines in *The Lord of the Rings* or his friend C. S. Lewis describes in *The Great Divorce*. These writers depict on a cosmic canvas the world's diverse inhabitants on a quest for true personhood. Their source, especially for Lewis, is Dante's *Divine Comedy*, which illustrates profoundly this journey into personhood. But why, we may ask, is this journey depicted in a phantasmagoric never-never land of allegory and characterization? I suggest that it is to heighten the dialectical tension of the human experience, which must extend beyond the material world for true personhood to develop. Yet a person can never strive directly for this growth. It comes about indirectly and inversely, in opposition to the world's way. Spiritual progress is actually material regress, and exaltation comes by way of humiliation. Christ's blessing appears in our being wounded, and weakness becomes the source of our strength. Thus the Christian's progress is offensive to the world because it is a total reversal of the world's understanding of success. Constantly the temptation of the Christian in the world is to collapse and eliminate the dialectic, to remove the offense of the cross, and to view the Christian life as one that is superficially positive, direct and straightforward.

Yet our own messy lives can be stranger than fiction, and our technological world has become global, like Dante's world, with cosmic consequences. Dante interprets hell as God allowing us to face the loss of all relationships as the consequence of our own perverted desires. Purgatory is the cleansing necessary to prepare us for right relationships. And heaven is where "the clean of heart shall see God" in the fullness of personal being. Dante did not write a text in systematic theology. His work is about the moral consequences of misused relationships, which we can all see around us every day. So we can readily accompany him on his journey.

Dante has several guides: Virgil (reason), Beatrice (love) and Bernard of Clairvaux (the joy of heaven), which are authenticated apostolically by Peter, James and John. But behind all of these is a seventh guide, the apostle Paul, whose blending of truth and love directs his pilgrim way through all the Scriptures. The Divine Comedy is perhaps the greatest Christian poem, its structure deliberately trinitarian with three-line stanzas (tercets) forming three major canticles, each containing thirty-three cantos. It is imaginative, moral and intellectual, concerned with beauty, goodness and truth; it spans past, present and future; and it is certainly focused on the Father, Son and Holy Spirit.

The poem is a kind of travelogue of five and a half days between Maundy Thursday and Easter Wednesday in about A.D. 1300, reflecting perhaps the poet's own pilgrimage to Rome that year. It draws on Dante's lifetime experience of knowing himself and interacting with contemporaries in Florence, as well as his wide reading at the height of humanistic Renaissance culture. The title Divine Comedy implies a blessed and joyous ending for the poet, who has personally experienced a healing vision of God.

More than a significant reading experience, I have found it to be a life experience that counters the narrowness of our technological society and even that of conventional Christendom. Instead of seeing thought or action at the core of our person, Dante, like Augustine before him, sees human desire as in vital need of both godly and intelligent transformation. Dante speaks for us, as well as for himself, in the recognition that without God, our desires are bankrupt. Human desire is insatiable, and unless it finds its terminus in God, we shall forever be tormented.

In the poem Dante Alighieri is thirty-five, a man of the world who at the height of his career was mayor of the great city of Florence. But he has been accused falsely of corruption. Condemned to death, now a fugitive in exile, he tells us,

> In the middle of our life's way
> I found myself in a dark wood
> Where the right path was lost.

He can see a path leading to a mountain, but it is barred by three wild animals, a lion (a symbol of narcissism), a leopard (arrogance) and a wolf (greed and rage). They all would destroy human relationships. So instead he is forced into the entrance of a cavern, accompanied by Aeneas, who also had visited the underworld.

Indecision is the vestibule into hell, and Dante finds a whole city of academics within its portals. Further in, the funnel into hell is divided into three great sources of human error: boundless lust, passionate violence and fraudulent greed. Hell is a journey into the loss of the self through contempt for others, a refusal to face the truth of oneself and a misunderstanding of freedom that leads to enslavement by obsessions and addictions. It is having to bear the consequences of our own mistaken desires. These mistaken desires begin with resentment. Eventually the lover of self becomes the hater of self. In hell's depths is Satan, frozen in the ice of impotent desire. The fallen angel, having desired infinitely for itself, can now desire nothing!

Dante finds it is important for us to "go to hell" with him in order to understand the consequences of his (and our) blindness, self-deception and pride. In hell he meets all the society he knew in Florence, but now he sees the consequences of their false desires with a stark clarity he didn't have before. Hell, he discovers, is where right relations with people and with things—sex, power, money, fame—are finally understood but can never be enacted. He sees the false roots of society, the church and his culture, and he finds many representatives of these in hell—even popes! It doesn't take much imagination for us to envision who we might encounter in hell: shopping mall crowds, boards of governors of prestigious institutions, stock market investors, sports fans, our neighbors in suburbia, yes, even ourselves. In essence, hell is anything that misdirects our desires from God so that we do not and cannot experience his love or share it with others. In hell divine love is simultaneously rejected and desired, and all contact with God is denied.

How does Dante get out of hell? He finds himself plunging further down, and naturally thinks he is going deeper into hell than ever before. Then he discovers he has gone through the center of the earth and sees the stars above him once more. Perhaps this reflects what a pastor once said in my class: "When you are at rock bottom, you will find Christ as the Rock at the bottom." Then we can experience, as Dante did, huge relief! Plunging into the enveloping darkness to reach the dark bottom is when you can look up, focused, to find your eyes now full of light.

Dante looks up to find himself on the mountain island of Purgatory. It has seven terraces on which souls are facing the consequences of the cardinal vices of their lives: pride, envy, anger, sloth, avarice, gluttony and lust. What is the purpose of Purgatory? It is where the desert fathers taught us we can "vomit the false self," facing our relational addictions and "drying out." To enter the desert of affliction is to find the highway of freedom away from our perversions. We do so by the three steps of contrition, confession and satisfaction; it is the process we call repentance.

Dante finds that as he ascends the mountain, love increases the more it is shared, becoming the motive to climb even higher. But sloth, or what the monks called *accedie*, is a prevalent discouragement, making the soul listless and weary in well-doing and hindering the process of liberation. The top of the mountain is reached when we overcome this discouragement and are freed from pride, ambition and willfulness. Then we see the divine relational panorama ahead of us, full of love, joy and peace. Here Dante falls into a deep sleep. What was insoluble in hell has become transforming in purgatory, resulting in a radical conversion. We can reinterpret our narrative, painful as it was, in the light of God's love. This gives us a wholly new perspective. A right relationship with God can re- √ deem all our other relations, both with ourselves and with others.

If technology challenges us to find focus at home, for Dante the focus is now heaven, where the heart finds rest in the coinherence of God's love. Heaven is truly our home. Dante had to go into exile and become homeless to learn this truth. We may need to be similarly broken, to be wounded by the God of Jacob as I have experienced myself. That is why I love the story Dante tells, for we do not understand our own narrative without first becoming homeless and then participating in God's love to see that in Christ "all things hold together" (Col 1:17). Dante's first great symbol is the funnel of perverted desires. Then there is the difficult mountain of humility, repentance and conversion. But heaven, or divine love, is symbolized as "the red rose" that "can no longer be kept closed," for the Christian person is designed to be an object of eternal beauty.

This icon of gracious fragrance is always open to the light, never closed within itself. Is it red because of the shedding of Christ's blood? Indeed, only in a sacrificial life do we find God at the center of everything. Then the beauty of heaven becomes indescribable, joyously passionate, ecstatic, literally taking us out of ourselves. Light, revelation, √ communion all flow into community, for our true personhood includes

all these dimensions of appropriating and participating in divine glory.
Now we see that love has been the purpose of the journey. Love can now
rest. No longer do we experience the loneliness of sinful, ambiguous relationships. We know even as we are known, says the apostle (1 Cor
13:12). Meanwhile Dante urges us to persist in our reading: "O you who
are of sound understanding, look at the doctrine that is hidden beneath
the veil of the strange verses."

Having read *The Divine Comedy* many times, T. S. Eliot wrote, "In the
end is my beginning, and in the beginning is my end." Dante descends
once more to earth, knowing the assurance of Paul that "in all things God
works for the good of those who love him" (Rom 8:28). Dante was the
first great poet to use vernacular language, assuring us that our ordinary
humdrum existence has eternal consequences. Becoming a person requires all the resources of heaven, but remaining self-centered carries the
hellish consequences of eternal damnation. In his famous sermon "The
Weight of Glory," C. S. Lewis echoes Dante in stating, "There are no ordinary people. You have never talked to a mere mortal." The awesome-
ness of people is depicted in the *Inferno* as immortal horror, in *Paradiso*
as everlasting splendor. It is not a light choice to make. I love Dante because he lifts my eyes to see that the journey toward personhood has infinite worth. And he says in *Paradiso*, "Anyone who sees that Light becomes a person who would not possibly consent to turn away to any
other sight; for the good that is the object of all desires is ingathered
there in its fullness."

When human beings are at peace with God, resting in his love, they
are uplifted to a dignity greater than anything the humanism of the Renaissance or our technological society could ever conceive. At the com-
pletion of Dante's *Divine Comedy*, we are reminded of the transformation
of which Paul speaks: "And we, who with unveiled faces all reflect the
Lord's glory, are being transformed into his likeness with ever-increasing

glory, which comes from the Lord, who is the Spirit" (2 Cor 3:18).

Thus did Dante share with the apostle Paul the belief that the Christian person reflects a newness of life that is essentially a new existence. Both inspire us to participate in the process of becoming persons in Christ. For the consequences are eternal.

PART 3

Maturing in Community,
Transmitting Faith in Person

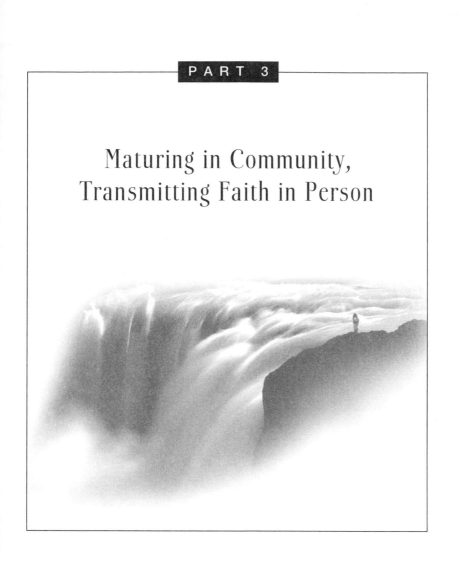

FIVE

Living the Truth in Love

The Reformation is characterized by exaggeration,
yet the things exaggerated—the need for independence of authority,
for freedom, for a real inwardness of belief—are of vital importance.
Those who were martyrs for it, as Bunyan partially was,
knew that it was mankind for which they were laying down their lives
or their liberties, and were prepared to suffer accordingly.

MONICA FURLONG
Puritan's Progress

If a man has any true love for God
he must have a spirit to love God above all;
because without seeing something of the divine glory
there can be no true love of God.

JONATHAN EDWARDS
Miscellanies

Of the things that followed I cannot at all say
whether they were what men call real or what men call dream.
And for all I can tell, the only difference is that what many see
we call a real thing, and what one only sees we call a dream.
But things that many see have no taste or moment in them at all,
and things that are shown only to one may be spears and
water-spouts of truth from the very depth of truth.

C. S. LEWIS
Till We Have Faces

*A*s Dante explored the love of God, progressing geographically on his pilgrim way through Italy and spiritually from the Inferno to Paradise, he must have often wondered if he was not going in the wrong direction. According to various passages in *The Divine Comedy,* Bologna was full of prostitutes and pimps, Florence was in league with the devil, Pistoja was a den of beasts and Genoa was utterly corrupt. Yet at the end of his journey, Dante finds love when, and where, God and man are united. Although he learned much from the great contemplative scholar Thomas Aquinas, who was in love with truth, Dante sought truth in order to love God. There is a difference between seeking to know things for the sake of knowledge itself and being willing to undergo renunciation to be possessed by the truth.

T. S. Eliot notes somewhere that "Shakespeare gives us the greatest width of human passion; Dante the greatest altitude and greatest depth," always setting the human scale before the presence of God. Dante considered Psalm 19 one of the greatest lyrics of the world. He recites in *Paradiso,* "The heavens declare the glory of God; the skies proclaim his handiwork," and then responds, "I seemed to see the entire universe smile, and I was enraptured by both sound and sight. O joy! O life of perfect love and peace! O endless, unlimited riches!" All paradise seems to ring with the sweet strain, "Glory be to the Father, to the Son and to the Holy Spirit!" For "the Love that moves the Sun and the other stars" directed the whole course of Dante's life—even when, in desolation over the loss of his standing before the world, he was unaware of God's presence.

Expressing our faith in narrative reveals that we are still trying to make sense of it all, to possess it. The narrative process allows our certainty to remain fluid, not rigidly cock-sure, and reflects our need for wider horizons and greater depths. Symbol and metaphor provide us with heavenly sky-hooks that allow a fuller and more personal integration of our faith but keep it still beyond our ken. Paradoxically, the broader the vista, the more hopeless the task of integration seems. Often I think faster than I can speak; I speak faster than I can act; and I have more actions than I can incorporate in my character. Consequently I need a greater unity and integrity of faith, while realizing that any progress God gives occurs at the slowest pace of all!

While we can speed-read theological knowledge and idealistically accept certain doctrines, faith invites us to commit our whole person in our everyday existence to living out the gospel of Jesus Christ as fully as possible. So we find that becoming Christlike progresses almost imperceptibly. For authentic integration we need to expect appropriate rates of apprehension, conversion and transformation. Like the psalmist, we will experience orientation, disorientation and reorientation as our emotions and desires are redirected and re-educated. Therefore we must maintain humility, gentleness, perseverance, fortitude, courage and especially patience with ourselves as we pursue the journey. As Dante experienced, the higher we climb, the rougher the way becomes.

THE OBLIGATION TO LIVE IN PRISON OR EXILE

For people who experience dramatic conversions, the change in becoming a Christian is clearly self-evident. But I had no such event in my life, and I have consequently interpreted most of my Christian life as taking place in a prison cell, hidden but hopefully not underground. God has used these images symbolically, helping me change slowly rather than giving me a Damascus road experience. Every Christian convert has the same obligation: to be different from the natural life we began at birth. For some of us the change occurs much more slowly, whether from pride, cultural blindness or the development of a more radical understanding the Christian life. For me, teaching at a theological college for more than thirty years has been an obstacle to change. Much knowledge remains secondhand, never properly digested as food for the soul. Similarly, the explosion of Christian literature today can contribute to religious illusion instead of authentic Christian living, remaining theory and not practice. I have already described this process as theological journalism, which reports data but does not live it out.

I vividly remember weeping within my soul as we marched ceremoniously in all our academic finery in Regent College's first convocation ceremony. It felt like I was ascending the scaffold to place my neck in the hangman's noose. Despite Samuel Johnson's remark that at such moments of lucidity "God mightily clears the head," it felt like a long imprisonment lay ahead of me. But in that moment Paul's words brought me immense comfort: "As a prisoner for the Lord, then, I urge you to live a life worthy of the calling you have received. Be completely humble and gentle; be patient, bearing with one another in love. Make every effort to keep the unity of the Spirit through the bond of peace" (Eph 4:1-3). Dramatic as his conversion had been, the apostle learned much from his numerous imprisonments. Only in prison, symbolic or physical, does one learn the true meaning of freedom: liberation from one's self. The Philippian jailor found Paul and Silas joyously singing psalms from within their prison cell. They did not need the earthquake that opened their prison doors; they were already profoundly free. Indeed, in writing to the Galatians, the apostle indicates that great moral consequences come from becoming enslaved to love: "Through love become slaves to one another" (Gal 5:13 NRSV). True freedom is the freedom to love others in spite of hostility. A great paradox of our Christian lives is that we can be most free precisely when we are also most frustrated. Encountering relational frustrations can angelically minister to us, helping us reach greater selflessness.

Exile has certainly been part of my family's narrative. My wife and I wrested our four teenagers from homeland and friends to restart life in a faraway land. A friend assured us confidently that our exile might indeed prove disastrous for us as parents but end up being the best thing for our children! Reflecting later, my wife and I realized that it certainly was the best way to instill resourcefulness and initiative in our children. But we have experienced too the powerful biblical motif of exile, which reveals God's larger purposes for all his people instead of allowing us to remain within our comfortable, narrow, self-focused point of view. Exile smashes our complacent perspectives, enabling us to see that restoration can only be found in God's hidden character, far beyond our pragmatism and control.

Jeremiah has been one of my favorite biblical characters since childhood, and I have often contemplated the Lord's words through him to the exiles: "Build houses and settle down; plant gardens and eat what they produce. . . . Also, seek the peace and prosperity of the city" (Jer 29:5-7). The hospitable life of shalom in the midst of discouragement is the way of life for those who hope in God. We look up to his holy temple and to his throne, and we look forward to his future kingdom when all will be restored in divine righteousness. The promise of a new age fills us with hope. Joseph discovered a truth similar to Jeremiah's. Being placed in a dark, deep well by his brothers was an experience God meant for good, regardless of his brothers' evil intent. When I have found myself at the bottom of a deep, dark well and looked up, my eyes were filled with light. Likewise, the dark well of exile prepared godly Israelites such as Simeon and Anna for the incarnation, the consolation of Israel. Exile can also prepare us over the long haul for unprecedented benefits.

THE CHALLENGE TO LIVE DIFFERENTLY

Knowing Christ is also finding strength in weakness. Paul carried the identity of being "a gynecological monstrosity," as Martin Lloyd Jones paraphrases, because he was "abnormally born" (1 Cor 15:8) and the chief of sinners (1 Tim 1:15). He lived a dialectical existence between weakness and strength, foolishness and wisdom, poverty and riches, shame and honor, slavery and freedom, suffering and comfort, frustration and glory, all of which he spells out in 1 Corinthians 4:7-17. This catalogue of sufferings is alienating, as all intense suffering is, but Paul's great cost was to give life to others. Likewise, we benefit others by dying unto the Lord Jesus so that his life may be seen in us. Exemplars such as Dante and Paul are not exceptional in this way; this role does not belong only to great mystics. On the contrary, all real Christians act out their witness through their dialectical experience of everyday life.

Yet when the apostle Paul writes "to the saints," we tend to envision a stained-glass piety that seems remote today. Even the word *holy*, which Wycliffe originally translated from the word *hagios*, feels distant to us, but essentially it implies difference. Israel was told, "Be holy [i.e., different] because I, the LORD your God, am holy" (Lev 19:2). Saturated as we are by our culture, we need to be reminded more than ever that being a Christian should make a real difference in our lives, behavior and sense of identity. Klaus Bockmuehl, a Regent colleague of mine, used to state radically that "the Ten Commandments is the basic contribution of the Christian church to public life." His nightmare was to find that an essay on the fourth commandment had been written by one of his students on a Sunday! Klaus saw the ethical obligation to "keep the Sabbath holy" as part of the identity of a true Israelite. Indeed, the seventy-year exile reflects Israel's failure to observe the Sabbatical years of the Promised Land. Consequently God has also given Christians a sabbatical identity. The

Christian should observe Sunday differently from the workaday schedule of the rest of the week and rhyme to a different timetable. Like circumcision, the Sabbath should remind us that God has given us a different identity than that of the world, for our being is profoundly in Christ, as we have discussed. Perhaps we still need periods of exile or imprisonment in our lives to help us reshape our fading sabbatical identity.

Likewise, the demand of the early church to maintain sexual purity before marriage should also mark the life of the Christian. The claim that we belong to God is at the heart of the apostle Paul's call for sexual purity among the Corinthians, so that when we exercise sexual license, we sin against God (1 Cor 6:12-20). We need to vocally uphold young Christians' chastity as a cause for joy. When peer pressure is strongest, practicing a different kind of sexual lifestyle from that of the world is a major event. But if there is no difference between the world's way of life and ours, then our credibility as Christians has gone. As we have seen, this is how so-called Christians contribute to the secularization of the world. The meaning of the term "sanctification," *hagiasmo,* is literally "the road to holiness," a path we tread for the rest of our lives.

CHRISTIAN SERVICE AND PERSONAL HOLINESS

Mark Strom, in his challenging book *Reframing Paul,* indicts evangelical culture for sharing in the same pagan abstraction, idealism and elitism as the Corinthian church of Paul's day. Much of this attitude arises from the elitist significance we have given to the role of the preacher, who monologues publicly instead of dialoguing privately in ordinary, gracious conversation. The importance we place on professional ministry and the unnatural way we have separated the ordinary life of marketplace Christians from the religious activities of the church generates a false elitism. In his book *Preacher and Cross,* Andre Resner asserts that a misunderstanding among Christians of the goals, norms and values of public ministry has resulted in a crisis in ministry. We have taken on the norms of the secular professional life, forgetting that the early fathers never separated sanctity from scholarship or Christian character from religious action. Christian scholarship cannot be egoistic. It must remain critical, but its purpose is also to be compassionate.

The poet George Herbert asks the question, "Lord, how can man preach thy eternal word?" In his moral inadequacy man is but "crazy, brittle glass," and yet in God's temple, he can become "a window through thy grace." For God can "anneal in glass" his story, "making thy life to shine within / the holy Preacher's." "Doctrine and life" can combine to penetrate the hearts of its hearers as well, something "speech alone" could never do. This mystery of divine communication through us as earthen vessels, despite all the advances of theological scholarship, will ever remain the mystery of godliness that Paul speaks of in light of the Trinity (1 Tim 3:16). Both preaching and personal conversation are vital to Christian witness, but we must not allow self-serving, intellectual or psychological connotations to dominate our communication about the mysteries of the Christian life.

Likewise, there is no such thing as "the psychology of Paul," if by that we mean that contemporary psychology can explain all the issues of the Christian life as exemplified in the apostle's life and ministry. Assuming that contemporary human consciousness was the same in the early church during late antiquity is anachronistic. Rather we need historical psychology to teach us how different the consciousness of previous generations has been, just as we appreciate that our cultural notions of self-identity have changed and are changing over time. For instance, whereas porosity of identity confused the boundaries between humanity and the gods in the classical world, with life constantly invaded by daimons as variable as the emotions, today our identity has become increasingly impermeable in self-centeredness.

Again, we may consider ourselves very discerning and naturally wise about the behavior of our fellow Christians, but we must exercise great caution not to disrespect the living out of their own personal faith in God. However discerning we may be, we can never wholly see through other people. Psychoanalysis, along with the intense skepticism it has created, has been wholly embraced by secular culture today, and it can be very damaging. Some of my most vivid memories of C. S. Lewis have to do with his constant concern in the early 1950s to distinguish between the need for a "clean window to look through in order to appreciate the view" and secular culture's use of psychoanalysis to look through everything, but which ends up seeing nothing.

Personal relations require us to attend to the particularity of the other. Uniqueness is a God-given gift of our personhood that we must celebrate in each other. Thus one of my inner habits has been to cultivate a prayerful attitude in the presence of other people, whispering inwardly, "Lord, make me reverent in the presence of this unique child for whom you died." Prayerfulness is the breath of relationship, an antidote to the godless poison of secular psychoanalysis. Prayer becomes intertwined with the desire to be indwelt by the Holy Spirit as we relate to others. It has a strong social character and purpose, expressed in supplication and intercession on behalf of others, and also a private purpose, contributing to our own spiritual formation. Indeed, I have found it impossible to separate prayer from friendship, as I expressed in the book *The Transforming Friendship: A Guide to Prayer*.

In pastoral care, which has been—and still is—a major focus of my life, I have seen the need for gentleness to be interwoven with frank confrontation. We find this in the apostle Paul's ministry. In 2 Corinthians 10:1 he writes, "By the meekness and gentleness of Christ, I appeal to you." The Corinthians saw in Paul's letters something very different from the humility they witnessed when face to face with him, for he wrote with a boldness they found threatening. So they concluded that Paul had a dual persona characterized by moral inconsistency. One of my favorite texts is Paul's confession, "Seeing then we have such hope, we use great plainness of speech," which contains both an eschatological and a pastoral element. Eschatologically, the reason for plain speaking is a redemptive hope of how God can redeem and transform us. Pastorally, Paul is just telling it like it is. Once a very attractive but unfaithful wife confessed her adultery to me, revealing that her grocery store manager was her illicit lover. "Oh, dear, what can I do?" she exclaimed. Bluntly I told her, "Shop in a different store!"

Paul even uses military metaphors to describe what the immoral Corinthians needed to see. They were engaged in moral warfare, so they needed spiritual weapons to demolish strongholds of temptations, to avoid being taken captive and to avenge disobedience (2 Cor 10:3-6). In pastoral ministry, being nice to people is not always a truthful way to help them grow spiritually. We must realize the radical nature of the Christian life. Indeed, as Jesus stated in Luke 14:26, we must exercise moral hatred—not as an emotion but as a godly conviction demonstrating the radical nature of our new life in Christ. A clean break with the past is essential to escape from our addictions, which are all symptomatic of idolatry. Hatred designates such a break with our past, demonstrating our summons to an eschatological newness of life that proves its credibility by proclaiming the boldness of the gospel without shame. Again, Paul's words in Romans 1:16, "I am not ashamed of the gospel, because it is the power of God," have meant a great deal to me, since I was naturally timid, fearful and self-apologetic in my youth.

WALKING ALLEGORICALLY WITH JOHN BUNYAN

Dante's contemporaries reportedly said of him as he walked down the street, "There goes the man who has been in hell." John Bunyan, after twelve years in prison, not only embodied the troubled times of civil war and religious conflict in seventeenth-century England, but like Dante also tells us terrible things about the human condition that we would rather not face in ourselves. His awareness of original sin, his personal honesty, his deep experience of divine grace, his realism about the temptations and trials of Christian life and his heavenly-mindedness still inspire us to walk the talk of the Christian faith. I read *Grace Abounding* and *The Pilgrim's Progress* as a boy, and I still read them.

Teaching a seminar on the Puritans and Cistercians with my colleague Jim Packer for almost two decades gave us the scope to see Bunyan in the context of Puritan monasticism and family life. But the metaphor of the soldier-pilgrim in Bunyan is also strong, allowing us to see his Christian identity as hard-edged, resolute and world-despising. He teaches us, as all the Puritans do, that the pursuit of godliness is not an exceptional effort and cause of great suffering, but the norm for every Christian. By trade a tinker, Bunyan walked many lonely miles between villages. As many of us have experienced, there were times when the Bible brought him no comfort. Bunyan fully understood the paralysis of guilt, and when the Song of Songs was opened to him expressing the love of Christ to his troubled soul, he then wanted to talk of the love of God "to the very crows that sat on the plow'd lands before me."

"Puritan" was a nickname given in mockery, but the Puritans themselves preferred the term "Precisian," for God is a precise God and his commandments are clear. But the Christian life can be flattened out too systematically and consequently become abstract and sterile. So the illiterate tinker John Bunyan did a daring thing. He expressed the Christian life in allegory. Anyone reading his works should start with his introductory apology for the use of allegory in matters of faith and conduct. Allegory allows us to see in all dimensions—depth and height, length and breadth—the contours of divine love revealed to us in Jesus Christ. Once we understand this, the exuberance, robustness and realism of Christian experience steps off the pages of *The Pilgrim's Progress*.

As a youth I wanted to be spiritual, but I was not. I wanted to be humble, but I was not. I wanted to be consistent, but I was a bundle of timid inconsistencies. But when I entered Bunyan's allegorical world I saw with new integrative assurance the whole drama being replayed vividly in my own life. Now the super-strategy of Satan's cunning and deceitful ways was exposed, and the cosmic consequences of being a Christian took on new clarity. The hard climb to "the Delectable Mountains," like Dante's Purgatory, leads us to a broader horizon of God's loving purposes.

The rigid literalism of many sectarians has often killed the communication of faith to succeeding generations. Today our franchised religious programs can produce the same result. But Bunyan argues, "Was not God's laws in older times held forth by Types, Shadows and Metaphors?" As the narrator of *Pilgrim's Progress* he falls asleep and dreams in a "den," which is actually a prison. Dressed in rags, he begins to feel terrible distress and weeping cries out, "What can I do?" He goes home to find that his family thinks he has gone crazy. But on a walk he meets Evangelist, who tells him he must set out through a gate in the field to escape the wrath to come. He cannot see the way, but he is told to set the distant light within his eye and to follow it. He seeks "Life, Life, Eternal Life." Soon he falls into the Slough of Despond, after which he meets Mr. Worldly Wiseman and then Legality in the village of Morality. Then, guided once more by Goodwill and passing over the Hill Difficult, he is refreshed in the House Beautiful. After that comes the terrible encounter with Apollyon in the Valley of Humiliation leading on to the Valley of the Shadow of Death and the town of Vanity Fair. He eventually finds himself and his companion Hopeful in Doubting Castle. After terrible sufferings there under the tyranny of Giant Despair and his wife Diffidence, they finally escape into the Delectable Mountains, cross the River of

Death and arrive at their heavenly destination. The story is amazingly dynamic and effective, and we can readily place ourselves in it, giving a vivid and deeper meaning to our own narrative.

Bunyan's protagonist, Christian, encounters or hears about some ninety characters. Seventeen are good, but the evil characters are by far the more realistic! Like the seven cardinal vices of the Middle Ages, there are seven categories of unreality that confront Christian: worldliness, pretentiousness, conceit, spite, lust, being easily led, and moral deadness. Sixteen characters reflect worldliness, followed by ten characters who are easily led. According to Bunyan, the real temptations of the Christian's journey are temptations to conform to the world. Bunyan, himself a nonconformist, was imprisoned for so long away from his young wife and four children precisely because he fought against worldly compromise. His faith took him far beyond the shallow waters of conventional religious life and into a deep ocean where profound contradictions are reconciled, providing buoyancy, exuberance and joy in the midst of intense suffering. Secularists like William James and Erich Fromm labeled him "poor, patient Bunyan" and even called him neurotic because they could not see the transcendent skyline of human and divine relationship. But the great poet and literary critic Samuel Taylor Coleridge saw otherwise. On the flyleaf of his son's copy of *The Pilgrim's Progress* he wrote:

> I know of no Book, the Bible excepted, as above all comparison which I according to my judgment and experience could so safely recommend as teaching and enforcing the whole saving Truth according to the mind that was in Christ Jesus as *The Pilgrim's Progress*. It is in my conviction incomparably the best Summa Theologia Evangelicae ever produced by a Writer not miraculously inspired.

HEAVENLY-MINDED MEDITATING WITH RICHARD BAXTER

G. K. Chesterton observed, "Our perennial spiritual and psychological task is to look at things familiar until they become unfamiliar again." Dante and Bunyan help us view our life more panoramically, which keeps us from spiritual complacency and moral sloth. In nurturing a passionate faith I have found the need, with symbolism and allegory, to cultivate a meditative way of life. Meditation breeds inner conviction, which in turn provides and strengthens consistency and equanimity of heart in the task of developing a more permanent Christian character. Like a vast system of underground streams, the Puritan movement of meditation in the seventeenth century began a renewal movement in the spiritual life of the church that has influenced it ever since.

Today I meet Christians who despair over the absence of reality in their faith because it was communicated to them cognitively and never allowed to develop emotionally. Even the pagan philosopher Plato distinguished four methods of gaining knowledge: reason, sensory experience, ecstasy and love. Our materialistic society understands the first two and ignores the second two. But Richard Baxter's classic *The Saints' Everlasting Rest* (1658) explores the roles of ecstasy and love through a meditation on Hebrews 4:9: "There remains, then, a Sabbath-rest for the people of God." This Sabbath rest, argues Baxter, is heaven. Consequently, practicing heavenly-mindedness for half an hour each day promotes the principle of "meliority": pursuing what is better in order to desire the best—heaven itself. The pursuit of heaven is the central spiritual dynamic of spiritual pilgrimage, because we seek something better than this world can give us. Unlike what Henry David Thoreau cynically thought, one world at a time is all a person can handle!

Yet we cannot live in perpetual restlessness since we are justified freely by God's grace, a truth affirmed by the biblical teaching that we are made in God's likeness and that he desires to reveal to us all he has, does and is. "If God is for us, who can be against us? He . . . did not spare his own Son," affirms the apostle (Rom 8:31-32). Rather than make us restless, this truth allows us to resolutely persevere in our pilgrimage toward a life that is, according to Milo Kaufman, "a future finer than dreams." The "pursuit of happiness" is simply a modern reinterpretation of classical philosophy. Heavenly-mindedness, on the other hand, is the fruition of a lifelong relationship with Christ in love, joy and peace. This is not a life of passivity or quietism, but of actively pursuing self-understanding in the presence of God and struggling against any inordinate attention to one's self.

There is a long medieval tradition of biblical meditation, or *lectio divina*, exemplified by writers such as Bernard of Clairvaux, William of St. Thierry, Jean Gerson and the writers of *devotio moderna*. Later, Richard Baxter, Richard Sibbes and John Bunyan carried on the work of encouraging Christian contemplation as a way to introduce a gleam of the eternal into ordinary life. Through meditation, joy becomes the anticipation of heaven and is incomparable to any other pleasure we can imagine. Other passions also remain important, such as a hatred of sin, zeal, compassion, shame and grief at our shortcomings. Prayer is the chief means of such consideration, of rational reflection along with thanksgiving for God's grace. Yet, ironically, modern Christians are more tempted to exercise yoga than to meditate on scriptural heavenly-mindedness!

If we need convincing, perhaps we should read C. S. Lewis's novel *Out of the Silent Planet*:

> [The hero Ransom] had read of "Space": at the back of his thinking for years had lurked the dismal fancy of the black, cold vacuity, the utter deadness, which was supposed to separate the worlds. He had not known how much it affected him till now—now that the

very name "Space" seemed a blasphemous libel for this empyrean ocean of radiance in which he swam. He could not call it "dead"; he felt life pouring into him from it every moment. He had thought it barren: he saw it was the womb of the worlds, whose blazing and innumerable offspring looked down nightly even on the earth with many eyes. . . . Older thinkers had been wiser when they named it simply the heavens—the heavens which declared the glory. . . . [This was] a more spiritual cause for his progressive lightening and exaltation of heart.

Lewis concludes his fantasy with the thought, "If we could even effect in one per cent of our readers a change-over from the conception of Space to the conception of Heaven, we should have made a beginning."

PURSUING GRACIOUS AFFECTIONS WITH JONATHAN EDWARDS

Another Christian guide I have greatly admired is Jonathan Edwards. Writing and preaching in a context similar to our own surreal culture, Edwards perceived that one of Satan's strategies is to fatally corrupt Christian life through the publicity of ecstatic expression. Edwards reminds us of the false political motivations inherent in our tendency to glory in public evangelical triumphalism. Likewise, is not the evangelical witness today losing credibility in becoming so politicized, perhaps not by the emotions, but by the entrepreneurial spirit? Even evangelical scholarship can become counterfeit if it overreacts too strongly to charges of fundamentalism and anti-intellectualism. Evangelical scholars sometimes wrongly affirm Jonathan Edwards as an icon for respectable religious intellectuals. This misuse of Edwards's classic *Religious Affections* (1746) is ironic indeed. Edwards's purpose was to teach the nature of God-given "gracious affections," which are neither falsely ecstatic nor, in reaction, falsely scholastic.

Edwards's text for his treatise is 1 Peter 1:8-9: "Though you have not seen him, you love him; and even though you do not see him now, you believe in him and are filled with an inexpressible and glorious joy, for you are receiving the goal of your faith, the salvation of your souls." The measure of our faith reveals itself in trials and not in success, for it needs to be tested. "True virtue never appears so lovely as when it is most oppressed," comments Edwards. Faith increases as it is purified. It expresses itself simply as love for Christ, nothing more nor less. It is unspeakable, for it is supernatural, ineffable in its excellence, God-given and God-inspired. "True religion, in large part, consists in holy affections," says Edwards in his most basic affirmation. Intelligent perception is a human faculty, but only God gives us the desire and inclination to reach out in true love for him.

From an early age, Edwards recognized that clarity about the things of God grows brighter when accompanied by a compelling desire to possess them in the heart. Only rebirth can produce a love for God. Only God's supernatural work within the believer can bring about true religious affections. These affections are not birthed objectively as the result of intellectual achievement or subjectively as an emotional state. In fact, self-deception works so deeply within us that valid affections for God are impossible unless they are bestowed by his grace operating on us.

God's beauty derives from his divine uniqueness, which distinguishes him from any other being. Likewise, our enjoyment of his beauty reflects a "gracious consciousness" different from any other form of consciousness. Others may speak abstractly of divine holiness, but only those possessed of God's Spirit can truly experience the beauty of his holiness. This experience cannot be achieved by human emotion alone. As Edwards says, "Gracious affections have their foundation out of self, in God and Jesus Christ." The Holy Spirit "sanctifies the reason, and causes it to be open and free."

Then the more a true saint loves God with a gracious love, the
more he desires to love him. . . . The more he hates sin, the more
he desires to hate it. . . . The more he longs after God and holiness,
the more he longs to long, and breathe out his very soul in longings
after God.

There is nothing ecstatically or intellectually egocentric about this
process. Edwards concludes that "gracious affections" are practical because we put them into practice on behalf of others, thus fulfilling the
double command to love God and our neighbor.

To speak of Christian experience and practice as if they were two
things properly and entirely distinct, is to make a distinction
without consideration or reason. Indeed, all Christian experience
is not properly called practice; but all Christian experience is
properly practice.

Just how costly it was for Edwards to live by these convictions is evident in his ouster from the church four years later in 1750. He was "cut
off in the ocean of the world" without salary, ten children to support, and
nowhere to go. Historian George Marsden interprets what went wrong
somewhat unsympathetically: "For someone who was known for his
analysis of the centrality of affections in religion, Edwards retained remarkably high confidence in the power of well-argued principle to pre-
vail." No! Marsden has misunderstood Edwards's interpretation of gracious affections. They are not about being tactful and politically nice to
people, but being biblically truthful. Yes, Edwards lived in the consciousness of a Newtonian universe, which was more rigid and fixed
than we now face in the fluidity of postmodernism. But the courage to
challenge human constructs of reality in any culture and historical period remains vital. Marsden concludes more wisely:

Edwards challenges the commonsense view of our culture that the material world is the "real" world. Edwards's universe is essentially a universe of personal relationships. Reality is a communication of affections, ultimately of God's love and creatures' responses. Material things are transitory and ephemeral. Their meanings are found in their relation to the loves at the center of reality. Although they are transitory, they can have great eternal significance if they are recognized for what they are, sign or expressions of God's love.

Being post-intellectual in our faith today implies neither anti-intellectualism nor intellectualism. It is more comprehensive than either of these extremes. It implies something more along the lines of the medieval idea of "holy folly," indeed, of becoming "fools for Christ's sake," as the apostle Paul stated (1 Cor 4:10). Christians throughout time have faced the task of communicating an identity that remains faithful to the gospel rather than to the world's idea of respectability.

Yet the complexity of life demands that we communicate in a variety of genres, as the Scriptures themselves do. Our faith needs to be expressed catechetically, narratively, poetically, prophetically, ethically and imaginatively. I smile now at my youthful arrogance when I felt tempted to believe that becoming a Christian meant having a reduced cultural life! For nothing stretches and challenges us— in mind, emotions, will and spirit—more than being a Christian. We conclude then with C. S. Lewis, who exemplifies so well as a Christian apologist the diverse genres we need today.

Seeking an Open Face with C. S. Lewis

I was privileged to meet regularly with Lewis between 1947 and 1953, when I shared an apartment with his friend Nicholas Zernov. We had frequent Saturday evening discussions in our home with a number of

Christian colleagues. After he left in 1953 to teach at Cambridge, I saw much less of him. So in 1957, thinking I might lose touch, l asked him what he thought his most significant message was as conveyed in his writings. He replied that *The Abolition of Man*, a collection of public lectures published in 1943, and his novel *Till We Have Faces*, published in 1956 to a disappointing response, best expressed his concerns. The former was a warning that an education based on moral relativism would produce a generation of "men without chests," mere technocrats unable to reason with their hearts. But the transformation of "an old batchelor" through his brief marriage to Joy Davidman, to whom he dedicated *Till We Have Faces*, helped him experience more profoundly the human transformation of the Christian identity through death and resurrection. Most studies of Lewis refer little to the novel, as the public ignored it in his lifetime. But he clearly felt that it expressed some of his deepest convictions. Why?

Lewis's friend and colleague J. R. R. Tolkien had coined the term *eucatastrophe* as a way to distinguish the Christian story from pagan mythic traditions. It is "the good catastrophe, the sudden 'joyous' turn. . . . It denies universal final defeat and in so far as it is *evangelium*, it gives a fleeting glimpse of Joy, Joy beyond the walls of the world, poignant with grief." For both writers, "myth" was not untruth but truth communicated through the imagination rather than through the intellect. It is about the inner world rather than the external world, fantasy expressed as a response to fallenness. It does not reduce truth conveniently to the shape and limits of our own minds. As Colin Duriez says, "The imagination, then, is concerned with apprehending realities (even if they belong to the unseen world), rather than with grasping concepts. So as a writer of fantasy, Lewis portrays the sense of otherness, a recognition of the numinous, a longing for joy, the understanding of art as sub-creation, and a yearning for recovery and healing."

In *Till We Have Faces* Lewis retells the classic myth of Cupid and Psyche. Orual, queen of the ancient kingdom of Glome, complains that in jealousy the gods have condemned her deep affection for her half-sister Psyche. Orual recounts their family life at the court of her father, King of Glome, doing so as truthfully as it is possible to do for the audience of the Greeklands, symbolizing the rationalistic character of their cognitive culture (such as academic life at Oxford reflected for Lewis). She does this under the tutelage of her Greek tutor, the Fox, who is a slave at the court. There arises a famine in the kingdom, and the angry gods demand that the youngest daughter of the King, Psyche, should be offered as the sacrificial scapegoat to appease their wrath. In this regard Orual voices what many popularly believe today, that the gods are the jealous rivals of human well-being. In contrast, Psyche willingly accepts her death, and afterwards, Orual discovers her beloved sister Psyche is not dead after all but gloriously happy in her new existence in "the divinely Other." For Psyche has now found true love, as she had never experienced before her own selfless sacrifice. Love has to be selfless to be truly "love." Orual had "loved" her sister falsely, as only self-love.

This throws Orual, now Queen of Glome in succession to her father, into ever greater anguish, assuming the gods have robbed her of Psyche's love. This parallels what people experience when their loved one becomes a Christian—the convert becomes enthralled with a greater lover! Psyche in freedom from the self stands in contrast to her half-sister Orual, the imperious ruler of her own kingdom who strives to maintain her prideful independence. Only when she in turn is broken to become reborn is she able to take off the mask that has hidden her ugly face, for now she has become beautiful. In dying and being resurrected she becomes like Psyche, gaining a face and becoming a real and full person.

This story is perhaps biographical, with Lewis as Orual and his wife, Joy, as Psyche. Joy too dies, and then Lewis discovers, as he quotes on the book's frontispiece, that "love is too young to know what conscience is." In a very different genre, Lewis like Edwards is telling us that gracious affections are not natural but have to go through the purification of death and resurrection. We need to identify such eucatastrophe in our own Christian narrative. The things that cause us the greatest personal suffering can actually free us from ourselves as we never imagined possible. As the poet Francis Thompson, after his long flight from the Hound of Heaven, discovers:

> All things I took from thee, not for thy harm,
> But that thou might find them in my arms.

SIX

Christian Transmission in an Age of Disjunction

Therefore, since we have such a hope, we are very bold.

2 CORINTHIANS 3:12

The knowledge of God without that of man's misery causes pride.
The knowledge of man's misery without that of God causes despair.
The knowledge of Jesus Christ is the middle course,
because in Him we find both God and our misery.

PASCAL
Pensées

What is of the greatest value is a good memory;
if this is wanting, [the Scriptures] cannot be of any great assistance.

AUGUSTINE
De Doctrina Christiana

Tradition receives bad press today, for the historical perspective has become dislodged by a more technical orientation. Yet as plants and animals require their ecological niches to grow and flourish, so human beings require tradition, both as their inheritance and as the means for

transmitting a living faith. Tradition is the whole environment of values and meanings into which a child is born and grows into adulthood. It is a place of teaching and practice, helping us learn from the past to live more creatively for the future. The apostle Peter speaks of the Christian's "new birth into a living hope through the resurrection of Jesus Christ from the dead, and into an inheritance that can never perish, spoil or fade—kept in heaven for you" (1 Pet 1:3-4). This inheritance or tradition is inherent in the Christian life, as Paul states: "For what I received I passed on to you" (1 Cor 15:3).

Ours is a historical faith based on events that actually happened to human beings in our space and time, not on abstract contortions of the mind. It is authoritative, not in power or external legitimacy but because it is given by personal trustworthiness. The root meaning of authority (Latin *augere*, "to make grow") is existential, implying that truth is passed on from one generation to another as a living, personal communication, not just a set of ideas. As Christianity expanded with the testimony of those who had known the risen Christ, believers would gather at the graves of martyrs, who as *traditores* had faithfully passed their faith on to the living. Celebrating the Eucharist together, dead and living were united in the faith. As Robert Wilken states, "The faithful departed were not simply remembered, they were welcomed as participants in the liturgy. . . . All the members of the church, past, present and future, were fused into one single community."

LIVING THROUGH CHANGE AND YET CONSTANCY

In my lifetime I have witnessed cultural changes of great magnitude. Having lived through the Depression of the early thirties, the Holocaust of which many were so ignorant while it was happening, and the Second World War, followed by the revolutionary disenchantment with modernism, I am bound to wonder what the future social shape of Christianity will be. Will Protestantism dissolve into ever-diminishing groups, with only those holding to apostolic succession having a lively enough tradition to pass on?

As Pascal faced the cultural changes taking place at the beginning of the modern age, he sensed that rational certainty was not enough. He had experienced that the living God of the Bible, the God of Abraham, Isaac and Jacob, can only be received by the heart in a relationship of faithful trust. What this transmission from heart to heart might imply for the church, Pascal did not live to tell us. His profound insights remained "thoughts" in an old shoebox. We have seen the same passionate fire in Kierkegaard, with his ultimate desire to experience the contemporary Christ, as exemplified by his prayer, "Lord Jesus Christ, may we too become contemporary with you; may we see you in your true form wrapped about with reality, just as you went about here on earth." Yet he also left us with only "philosophical fragments," as he called his efforts against Socratic reasoning.

What both Pascal and Kierkegaard imply in their communications is that Christ is contemporary only to the poor in spirit. We must see the cosmic abyss of the fall of man on the one hand in order to witness the redemptive grandeur of human destiny in the grace of the living God. Every point of time is equidistant from eternity. Only in realizing this can we see how contemporary Christ really is, and then also how tangible eternity can be to us now. We also need to identify and associate with unexpected contemporary friends of Christ to be invigorated by his daily presence in the lives of others, sometimes from ecclesial traditions wholly different from our own.

My first public address at the opening of Regent College was based on the dialectic theme of the writer to the Hebrews: "Jesus Christ is the same yesterday and today and forever" (Heb 13:8). Truly he is the unchanging Christ. Yet he is also the onward-going Christ, beckoning us to follow him in faith beyond the city walls of human achievements and our own limited horizons, to step "outside the camp" (Heb 13:12-13). We encounter vicissitudes and contingencies in life in order to meet him in our weaknesses, dry spells and sorrows as our true contemporary, the man of sorrows acquainted with grief (Is 53:3). We may meet him in unexpected people as well as unexpected places. We may even meet with him in people we never imagined were Christians. There he may communicate to us that he is the Reality beyond all our conceptions of reality.

In terms of inverse dialectics, we must be prepared for a faith of double vision. The tension of this double vision involves our affliction and suffering for our belief in what the world calls absurd, yet at the same time experiencing the blessedness of eternal life. Faith is not merely believing against popular understanding. It is accepting a way of life that is both triumphant and victorious, and yet also one of hardship and defeat. So we rejoice with those who rejoice and weep with those who weep.

Indeed, we are more likely to see things from God's point of view when our natural expectations are shattered by suffering and replaced by a new construct of reality. Our afflictions teach us what it is to have the mind of Christ. But if in avoiding suffering and offense we give our own cleverness and autonomy free rein to win the world's applause, we obliterate Christ's presence. We live in denial of our sinful condition, becoming helpless addicts who skate and fall over the surface of things. Likewise, if we avoid the depths of human tragedy we also miss the magnitude of Christ's love. Christian suffering is like a musical undertone deeper than any bass instrument can produce in a symphony. It is, in fact, completely different from the world's suffering, always redemptive in its results, whereas natural human suffering can be self-destructive, in despair leading even to the advocacy of "mercy-killing." But in Christian faith, the deepest affliction can shine through tragedy and transform it.

LIVING WITH CONTEMPORARY FRIENDS OF CHRIST

Who can deny that the soul of the Russian people has known suffering and the agony of oppression? My early friend and fellow Oxford lecturer Nicholas Zernov came to England as a refugee and lived as an exile. When I told colleagues we shared accommodation together, the response was often, "You must have an opaque soul!" For it was well known that Nicholas lived transparently with a radiant face in spite of his poverty and the educational handicaps of his youth. Instead of living in survival mode, inattentive to others because of his own basic needs, he developed a remarkable ability to enter the hearts of his friends. Late in life he reflected,

> Friendship brings a new dimension into human relationships. The notion of "another" (Russian *drugoi*), which combines both similarity and difference, reveals the essence of friendship. In a friend (*drug*) we find someone who is close to us in spirit, with thoughts and experience in tune with ours, yet not as a double, nor as someone identical to us.

Nicholas opened such prospects to me, providing "that lofty freedom of the soul" (as poet Anna Akhmatova put it) that enables others to be unafraid to be! Even more than friends such as Nicholas, the apostle Paul has long inspired me as a friend through his letters. His remarkable boldness for the gospel is expressed in his words, "Seeing then we have such hope, we use great plainness of speech" (2 Cor 3:12 KJV). So like Nicholas and Paul, I have sought to get down quickly to "gut issues" with other people, believing that God is able to do exceedingly above all that we ask or think. With such hope we can help others open themselves up to receive the boldness of faith.

Nicholas also introduced me to Dostoyevsky shortly after he had published an appreciation for him in *Three Russian Prophets*. I learned from

Nicholas how brilliant a psychologist Dostoyevsky was in depicting the
deep caverns of the human condition, as we saw in the first chapter. Dostoyevsky sees his characters "standing on the edge of a precipice of crime
and degradation, and yet they long for goodness and truth. Their whole
life is a struggle; they are torn between their hopes and fears. Love and
hate, a readiness to help and a desire to hurt constantly contest in them."
Later, I came to see Christians also dwelling in this world of the gro-
tesque depicted in Dostoyevsky's novels. Certainly he brought to an end
the naïve optimism surrounding "the progress of man," even though as
Christians we don't always get the message, making as we do so many
unrealistic claims for what our ministry can accomplish. The increasing
cry I am hear from Christians now is how inconsistent is the practice of
our faith when we place such an emphasis on a personal relationship
with Christ while remaining so impersonal with each other.

With the Enlightenment, the social sciences interpreted reality as general, displacing the individual and ignoring the historical component.
They have generalized about the human condition ever since, disregard-
ing historical specificity and personal narrative. As the poet W. H. Auden
ironically remarked, "Thou shalt not sit with statisticians, nor commit a
social science." Fortunately, this is a situation some contemporary ther-
apists seek to rectify. But ideologies such as socialism went further, denying God in order to ground reality on the earth. This is where Dostoyevsky expressed such psychological mastery in his characters. Diane
Thompson comments on his last and most brilliant novel, *The Brothers
Karamazov,*

> Dostoyevsky is both a realist in the usual sense and "realist in the
> higher sense." He could create vivid images of reality (the "earthly
> show") and then, with a sudden turn of phrase . . . he could turn
> them into images of "eternal verity." He combined reality so seam-

lessly with Reality that we cannot tear them apart without doing violence to the artistic integrity of the whole novel.

As Dostoyevsky writes to a friend, "There is nothing more realistic than these themes," (*i.e.* human immortality, the existence of God, our encounter with Christ and living in God's world). So his writing, he continues, "won't be like a sermon, but a kind of story, a tale of actual life. If it succeeds, I shall have done something good: I will force people to realize that the pure ideal Christian is not something abstract, but is graphically real, possible before our eyes, and that Christianity is for the Russian Land the only refuge from her ills." In Christ Dostoyevsky saw that the ideal and the reality were the same. He chose the monk Father Zosima to be the Christian realist, in contrast with the worldly Grand Inquisitor, the unreal Machiavellian theorist of religion.

I was given further insights into *The Brothers Karamazov* by a saintly neighbor and friend of Nicholas Zernov, Nadejda Gorodetzky. Her book *Saint Tikhon of Zadonsk: Inspirer of Dostoevsky* helped me appreciate the novelist's Christian historical ideal. Born Timofey Sokolov in 1724, Tikhon was nominated bishop of Voronezh, resigned four years later, and lived as a monk until his death in 1783. Of him Dostoyevsky said, "If only I could depict a positive holy figure . . . Tikhon, whom long ago I received with great delight into my heart." Dostoyevsky appreciated that true sanctity lies in deep yet selfless individuation, so he added, "The most important thing about Tikhon is Tikhon."

The theme of Dostoyevsky's novel is that denial of God needs to be confronted by the best of the Russian people, as represented in his novel by the saintly Orthodox figures Father Zosima and Alyosha. But Tikhon differed from Dostoyevsky's literary characters in that he was no Slavophile, and he had no Russian messianic mission. Rather he was a simple believer, childlike in his trust of Christ, lover of Paul's epistles, his eternal viewpoint so focused that to die was simply to embrace heaven. The theologian Fr. G. Florovsky writes that Tikhon's book *True Christianity* "was a first [Russian] attempt to formulate living theology, experimental theology in distinction, and as a counterbalance, to the schools devoid of authentic experience." He was the first Russian writer to offer religious instruction to the family, and he loved little children. He begged adults to watch their speech and behavior with children so as not to wound the souls of the little ones.

So Dostoyevsky portrays the ideal Christian as a specific spiritual director, Tikhon, represented in *The Brothers Karamozov* by Father Zosima, whose influence is still alive a century later portraying the mystery of the Christian living continuously with the resurrected Christ. As Father Zosima says to his disciple Alyosha, "Much on earth is concealed from us. But in place of it we have been granted a secret, mysterious sense of our living bond with the other world, with the higher heavenly world, and roots of our thoughts and feelings are not here but in other worlds."

Father Zosima narrates in his story that as a young military officer he challenged another officer to fight a duel to uphold his honor. But the night before, he had a vision in a dream that he should not fight the next day. So he stood before his enemy to die by being shot; his opponent missed. But instead of using this opportunity to kill his enemy, Zosima walked away from the duel, resigned his commission and became a monk. People both laughed at him and loved him as someone with a secret in his soul who could be trusted unreservedly.

This is the ambiguity of the Christian life, to combine narrative with vision. We are told, as Alyosha was told, "Yours will be a long pilgrimage," for it is a journey between vision and narrative, love and laughter, dream and debate, trust and disbelief, heaven and earth. When we live with *dramas sub specie aeternitaris*, facts are not what matter but the motives behind the facts. As Simone Weil observed after her conversion,

"The tree is not rooted in the earth, but in the sky!" Or as the apostle prays, "That you [may be] rooted and established in love" (Eph 3:17), divine love, which indeed is in heaven above!

Orthodox theology stands apart from Western Christianity in that it did not contribute to the rationalism of the Enlightenment. Its apophatic theology may tend to weaken ethical responsibility, but it has never separated the personal experience of divine mystery from the dogmas of theology. As Vladimir Lossky puts it, "The dogma which expresses the divine truth and appears to us like an unfathomable mystery must be lived in such a way that, instead of assimilating the mystery to our manner of understanding it, we must, on the contrary, strive to bring about a profound change, an inner transformation of the soul, so that we will be more receptive toward mystical experience." This is what Father Zosima contributes to our understanding of life in Christ: a conjunction of vision and narrative.

THE CRISIS OF CHRISTIAN TRANSMISSION TODAY

"Where there is no vision, the people perish" (Prov 29:18 KJV). Since the essence of education is to engage in transmission, a crisis arises when there is no vision for a future narrative. The vision of mortality should be a strong motive for transmission. Without assurance of the afterlife, the Israelites had only the hope of being remembered by their children and future generations. For them transmission was a substitute for resurrection. Many of us are still comforted to have some assurance that our children's children will continue in the ways of the Lord.

Vividly I remember the threat of the Cuban missile crisis in 1962, when the prospect of a nuclear holocaust seemed very real. I date my own commitment to the next generation from that point, when I became determined with God's help to act as compassionately as I could for young people. Perhaps the global crisis launched a new radicalism of the human spirit, which has since taken many forms, including a revolt against rationalism. Certainly it helped me think radically about what Christian education might become as we began to dream about the founding of Regent College.

The crisis of Christian transmission is part of a larger issue: the loss of a historical consciousness, the distrust of traditional authority, the implausibility of institutions, the autonomy of the individual and above all the loss of the fear of the Lord in a technological world. The breakdown of the family, the experimentation with new models for the family unit, the changing role of women in society and the diverse forms of sexual revolt all negate any continuity in religious transmission. Instead a new model is arising, which can be called "believing without belonging." In the Roman Catholic church and major Protestant denominations, transmission has traditionally been sociologically based, generating and perpetuating a religious culture. The revolt of women against traditional cultural mores of sex and procreation has led to the breakdown of the motherly role as primary transmitters of religious family values. Catholic sociologists in areas such as Italy, Spain, France, Germany and Latin America see this as a dramatic break with the past, especially during the last three decades. And a French Catholic writer has recently asked in the title of his book, *Are We the Last Christians?*

Perhaps, then, it is in this period of history that we need to recover a theology of exile. For like Jeremiah and the other prophets, exile is our cultural environment as well. When we live in a socially friendly world, we take transmission of faith for granted and do not pass it on as deliberately. When the social environment is more hostile, real Christian transmission must become more personal.

Christian witness today appears to be at a crossroads. The great majority of Christians still believe in institutional and social transmission of faith and cannot imagine Christianity being anything other than that currently conceived of by religious organizations, public churches, theological colleges, conferences and all manner of mission enterprises. Yet much of their effort is contributing to what we have called the surrealism of public ministry, with its focus on mass communication. When transmission is more intimate, it demands a personal experience of God that is responded to radically, and therefore felt more deeply in one's innermost being. Then it is exercised more relationally and reflects a holistic life of faith and trust.

In the past, church members commonly assumed that the most intimate experience of God was reserved for the priest, pastor or Christian leader. It was assumed that ordinary Christians did not participate much in transmission. Perhaps the words of our Lord were not deeply understood: "I praise you, Father, Lord of heaven and earth, because you have hidden these things from the wise and learned, and revealed them to little children" (Mt 11:25). The temple system of Judaism had indeed "hidden these things" from the simple people to whom Jesus spoke and transmitted his love. Yet "each of us has one Master, who dwells within each of us," as Augustine recognized. Each of us is directly responsible to Christ, and each of us needs nurture and guidance to make the transmission of faith more intimate. This requires self-understanding in the light of a deepening understanding of God and experience of the reconciling character of the gospel in our relationships and emotions. It demands awareness that to live realistically is not only to live in this world but also to accept the reality of the living, personal God. Through his Spirit we can walk with him intimately in the light of the resurrection and ascension of Jesus Christ. But institutionalized religion tends to take away the offense of such a double reality and to replace the presence of the Holy Spirit with its own pragmatism.

As the modern world perishes, we still need to transmit basic human values in spite of our cultural disjunction. I can see a new "redoubt" mentality taking over in the so-called free world. As secularization sweeps over the northern hemisphere, the demographic locus of Christianity is moving to the southern hemisphere. This is also producing a loss of metaphysical moorings so that, as Dostoyevsky predicted, if God is dead, then everything is permitted. Globalism is leading to major uncertainties, and the loss of a historical past is blinding us and reducing us to a merely technical consciousness. These trends are removing all our familiar landmarks.

TRANSMISSION AS CLASSICAL *PAIDEIA*

Recently this crisis has motivated a group of educational philosophers to promote "the *paideia* project" as a recall to classical civic education. Originally, the word *paideia* referred to the disciplined education of privileged families in the Greek city-state. Sons were individually tutored in a prolonged holistic process to become good and informed citizens. Motivating this process was the supposed visionary tutelage given by the mythical gods to humans—for instance, Athena's instruction of and care for the Athenians as patroness of their particular culture.

But the rapid expansion of the Hellenistic empire by Alexander the Great, analogous to globalization today, created an unimaginably expanding scale of existence. So the wise Hellenistic man (such as Cicero) had to reconceive himself as a citizen of the world, not just of a small city community. As Plato put it, the individual culture imparted by Hellenistic education—to make man the measure of things—now seemed "the most precious boon granted to mortal man," for it was "the good" worth having for the rest of life. If the *paideia* education was, and still is, focused on civic interest, what of the early Christian response to it?

The New Testament writers living in this *paideia* culture took personal tutelage further—much further. They pointed to the vision of Jesus Christ as our unique *Paideia*. Indeed, the promise of Christ was that the

Holy Spirit would become the disciples' divine Paraclete, acting in their lives as their *Paideia*. This irrevocable commitment to Christ and to the abiding presence of the Holy Spirit later led the desert fathers to establish their unique way of life, and then the medieval monks to monasticism. As contemporary Christians our commitment can seem pale in comparison, so some of us are now seeking more intense, individual guidance— perhaps from a mentor, soul friend or spiritual director—to become more serious about our calling. For if our evangelicalism is more politi- cal than radical, we become casual about our faith, inconsistent, schizophrenic and false. In that case we need not be surprised when the transmission of faith becomes unsustainable in the next generation.

For the early church, as well as for the family, there were two sources of instruction in the faith: personal and communal. The apostle Paul was much concerned with how parents educated their children (Eph 6:4; Col 3:21), and the early churches appointed teachers to educate new converts (Acts 13:1; 1 Cor 12:28; Eph 4:11). By the end of the first century, the term "Christian education" was in use by Clement of Rome. Later, Chrysostom elaborated on how parents should teach their children, suggesting that the family meal was a good place to begin. By the end of the second century, the church required a long probationary period of three years for the instruction of baptismal candidates in the faith. Augustine of Hippo later elaborated on "how to begin religious instruction." All Christians, however, were trained individually until the end of late antiquity. According to H. I. Marrou, Christian schools as such did not develop until the Middle Ages. Perhaps we need to revert to the original, more personal model, which combines the vision and narrative of the death-resurrection-ascension of Christ that is so radical to the Christian life. There can be no commitment without transmission, nor indeed transmission without consistent commitment.

I experienced a challenge to answer such a call in the early 1960s, when an Oxford student from a missionary family told me that his faith seemed irrelevant and meaningless. Moreover, he was in love with a non-Christian woman and thinking of marriage. I pledged that I would lunch with him every Friday, which I did for a year. Rational argument seemed useless, for he "knew it all," but he was vulnerable to the constant prayers on his behalf, the commitment and love of Christian friends, and his own bleak inner loneliness. Still unconvinced, though, he volunteered to do meteorological work at the South Pole, where he was almost literally alone with God, able to receive and send mail only once a year.

After two years he came home a transformed man, devoutly committed to Christ and on his way to becoming an important Christian leader. This event deeply encouraged me to continue the constant exercise of earnest supplication on behalf of others in the context of sustained loyalty and trust, and the commitment to "walk the canyon floor" alongside others in their distress. We really cannot pray for others when we are inconsistent, shallow, unkind and unsympathetic in relationships. Nor can we transmit the values we say we believe in without the truth dwelling richly in us and expressed outwardly in empathy and mutuality.

My father dearly loved the idea that "Enoch walked with God" (Gen 5:22), which was engraved on his tombstone. This led him to reflect on how other founding fathers of faith did likewise. For Noah walked with God (Gen 6:9), and then Abraham was invited to walk before El Shaddai (Gen 17:1). These personal experiences developed into symbols of the covenant life of Israel, through the exodus into the Promised Land and then through the exile as well. The guiding light of this journey of faith was the fear of the Lord, the basic principle of wisdom that led to an integrated life of experiencing God.

Guides for our own visionary journey need to be similarly committed to the covenant life, both inwardly and outwardly. For if wisdom is the effective application of knowledge to life situations, then it cannot tolerate discrepancy between thought and action, word and deed. The wise instructor must have godly integrity. This is what my father exemplified to me, causing me to want to show others the same thing. It helped me to see that fatherlessness is a major cause for much cultural schizophrenia, in which a generation of Ishmaels wander the world, unsheltered in a moral desert.

Scholars disagree over whether Jesus' use of "Abba, Father" was unique in Israelite prayer life. But of course it was! Only the Son of God can uniquely give us boldness to say the Lord's Prayer, for he alone can teach us to pray. For many years I dwelt on the clauses of the Lord's Prayer, which helped shape the meaning of spiritual sonship for me. Sonship leads us to understand discipleship, given such prominence in the Gospels as being taught by our divine Master. Yet each New Testament writer presents in different contexts a diversity of expressions of such transmission, within the continuity of the same gospel. So too, today, each of us must be flexible enough to meet every context and contingency so that we keep the transmission alive and enlivening of others. The dialectics continue as this but also that, for the more we dwell in the Beloved, the more playful we can be with the paradoxes of the Christian life.

We can be like the psalmist, living fully with the complete range of our emotions, at times complacent, then painfully disoriented, and later deeply redirected. We also live with the daily rhythms of the seasons of the year and of life, and with the sacred calendar of God's entry into our world. Just as we are characterized as humans by many recurrent rhythms, breathing in and breathing out, sleeping and waking, eating, drinking and abstinence, loving and procreating, nurturing and giving freedom to our children, so too we are shaped spiritually. For we are nourished by the Eucharistic meal and by the celebration of Epiphany, Advent, Lent, Easter, Pentecost, Ascension and All Saints' Day. Our identity is truly a sabbatical identity, so that one day in seven we cease from our secular workaday world to acknowledge our Creator-Redeemer. Pastors lead us forward year by year in reinforcing the reality of the divine revelation to conform and transform us into Christ's image. In turn our children watch and imitate us, repeat the same family rituals and continue to walk in the ways of their fathers. But if the spiritual rhythm is broken temporally, or weakened morally by inconsistency, the links with the past will not be sustained.

Oral transmission was pivotal to Israelite life, even when it became a literate culture. Whether the one reading the sacred text was priest or father, the act of orality remained personal. The oral tradition of preaching also gave us a rich heritage, along with the printing press, for we can still enjoy the compelling sermons of John Donne, the Puritans, John Wesley, C. H. Spurgeon and many others. Even the cantatas of Bach were composed to fit into the sermon and freshly delivered each Sunday, hence their vitality and variation. But these means of transmission remained in a national framework until contemporary secularization began to grow globally.

TRANSMISSION BY A SPIRITUAL GUIDE

The spiritual father, or *staretz*, that Dostoyevsky depicted as Father Zosima, transmits faith by example. If you desire to be such a guide, observe the face of someone you trust, for our faces can often put others off. Then observe his or her kindness, how this person provides space for the directee to gain self-insight. As Kallistos Ware, academic successor to Nicholas Zernov, puts it, "The task of the spiritual father is not to destroy a man's freedom, but to assist him to see the truth for himself: not to suppress a man's personality, but to enable him to discover himself, to grow to full maturity and to become what he really is."

The spiritual guide is a doctor, counselor, intercessor, mediator and sponsor. As a doctor she treats the sickness of sin, facilitating confession to help purge the poison within. Compassion provides healing for the pain of the soul, and a proper diagnosis gives the patient hope. As a counselor, the spiritual mentor helps clarify confused emotions and speaks an appropriate a word of insight and redirection. The intercessor pleads in the name of Christ for deliverance, reconciliation, renewal and newness of spirit. Christ alone is our mediator, but the soul friend can share in the participation of Christ in a tangible relationship. And as sponsor, the spiritual director is a burden bearer (Gal 6:2), helping to carry the cares and sorrows of the one weighed down.

The gift of discernment, or *diakrisis*, is vital for all this soul care. Without a selfless attitude it is impossible to provide true guidance, since listening in discernment requires us to enter into the heart of the other and accept his or her uniqueness. The essential goal is to share the life that is hidden with Christ in God in such a way that the truth is communicated in love, in the presence of God's Spirit, who links our lives mutually in divine participation. If this seems mysterious, visionary indeed, then some practical insights may help.

In seeking to create effective personal relationships, none of us is wholly objective, pure or innocent. Yet this deficiency can give us a "rearview mirror" awareness. When we overreact emotionally to negative offenses, we begin to see that our oversensitivity is often due to wounds from past relationships. In this process we can gain greater self-understanding; indeed, we begin to see that all our present relationships reflect our entire relational history. Deeper self-understanding can help us become more socially sensitive and wise. It can even help us recognize why we may react negatively to exhortations to "read the Bible" or "say our prayers." We may be remembering the negative feelings we used to associate with the rigid devotional life of our parents or a Sunday school teacher who was stern and even unkind.

In giving people advice about what they should do, we waste a lot of effort if we don't discern the inner gravity of their situation and what causes them pleasure or pain. Understanding human motivations and why people are driven as they are helps us discern their behavioral addictions at one end of the spectrum and potential effectiveness at the other. Yet we need to resist making hasty judgments that stereotype. It is beneficial to listen to others always in a spirit of prayerfulness, reminding ourselves of the unique identity God gives each one of us. We also must resist the tendency to assess people too functionally, as is our inclination in a technological world. It is not God's plan for us to live as cogs in a cosmic machine.

In acting as spiritual guides, we also should keep in mind that compensatory behavior is often praised by our society. People may perceive our efforts as gifts and strengths when they really reflect our attempts at self-redemption. For example, as a lonely child I compensated by becoming an absorbed reader, and later I became a successful scholar. Someone else may feel unnoticed and so become extroverted, acting publicly to claim attention. People who are altruistic and nurturing, or assertive and decisive, or analytical and self-directed, or flexible and coinhering may be overcompensating as a result of their personal narrative, with their strengths relapsing into weaknesses of character. In these scenarios we act as our own redeemer, only to discover that our behaviors are not life-giving to others, however much we succeed in public life. In contrast, Paul's theology was, "When I am weak, then I am strong" (2 Cor 12:10). In weakness we are more likely to seek God's help and channel his grace to others because we realize that the source is divine and not human. When Proba, the wealthiest woman of the Roman empire, asked Augustine, "How do I pray?" he reminded her that she was a widow, and true prayer comes from being a spiritual widow—destitute and in need of God's help. All true pray-ers are spiritual widows.

In this process we discover that our weakness can be the compass for our spiritual journey. When Christian in *Pilgrim's Progress* admits that he does not know the way, he is instructed to fix his eye on the light and to follow it. Likewise, our ability to be divinely guided arises from our uncertainty, our inadequacy, our doubts and fears. Instead of denying or ignoring our basic weaknesses, in them we seek God's redemptive grace most passionately. As we limp along on our spiritual journey, our compass points to where God's grace can meet our deepest need, transforming it into gracious strength. Like a light we set our eye on it, and we move forward. Through acknowledging our behavioral addictions, we can be transformed by the intimacy of Christ. Indeed, Samson's riddle can give great hope to the despairing: "In [the lion's carcass] was a swarm of bees and some honey" (Judg 14:8). Nothing is more ferocious and deadly than the king of beasts, and yet nothing is sweeter and more nourishing than honey!

Spiritual friendship is friendship in the company of Christ. It is not just giving good advice, though we all need wisdom in the application of the gospel to daily life. Rather it is like being an accompanist, a teacher playing along with her pupil and giving the music greater range and quality. Prayer is another form of accompaniment, as someone who has a long familiarity with the Eternal Friend inspires the beginner toward a long life of communion with God. Then, whether we are in desolation or consolation, the whole gamut of our emotions, aspirations and commitments can all be interwoven by Christ into a new song. The soul friend gives guidance in what the Puritan Robert Bolton called "a comfortable walking with God." Taking this literally, I have found that a good place to begin with a shy counselee is to take an early morning walk together. We walk symbolically, too, sometimes in the garden, other times in the desert, or even—and this is where we need our spiritual friends the most—in the dark night of the soul.

MEMORY AND THE PSALMS IN AUGUSTINE

All throughout this collection of reflections is the shadow of Augustine. While he was not the originator of the genre of autobiography, he enlarged his own personal interiority by remarkably engaging with the Psalms in a way that few have done before or since. For more than twenty years he preached weekly on the Psalter, and he reflected on it daily. According to Augustine, humans relive the Psalms, experiencing personal continuity and further self-knowledge through the memory of them. This involves fitting meaningful biblical episodes into our own personal narrative. These episodes make sense in our present situation but also strengthen the values we desire to experience ever more fully in our lives.

True autobiography then is not the chronology of good times and bad times, nor a record of the incidents and achievements of the self. Rather, as Augustine expresses in his *Confessions,* it is the narrative of ethical choices made at the crossroads of one's pilgrim way, along with choices already made by the Psalmist, which we can follow or else pay the consequences. It is the recollection of points of irrevocable departure. It is writing about things that have no literary appeal unless they have been lived personally. So Augustine interprets memory both as a state of being and a state of becoming.

Of course, he is not unique in this regard, for the apostle Paul in his letters had already developed this autobiographical approach in his nurture of Christian believers. Paul's memory had been full of the Scriptures, trained as he was in the famous rabbinical school of Gamaliel. But when he encountered the risen Christ, he realized that the law was incapable of redeeming humanity without the death, resurrection and ascension of Christ. Now the righteousness of God as revealed by Christ Jesus was operating apart from the law. The memory of Paul's conversion transformed all he had previously known of the law, the Messiah, the Psalms and the promises of the Old Testament prophets. The memory of his conversion shaped his entire future.

The apostle had been "a Pharisee of the Pharisees," a fully absorbed religious reformer, until he realized he was on the wrong track. Augustine had been an eloquent rhetor, using words and speech with great fluency, but he too discovered that life is not about human accomplishments. Rather it is revised, rewritten and redefined in the presence of God. The narrative becomes different as the narrator changes. Narration for narration's sake becomes transformed by the experience of a new, visionary life. Memories can disintegrate with lack of use, or they can be reshaped by the use made of them. As Augustine observed, "Just as I have a memory of past remembering, so in the future, I shall be recalling it by the power of memory." It is the experience of remembering that becomes significant.

In *The Testimony*, Augustine observes that "we cannot properly say that the future or the past exist or that there are three times, past, present, and future. Perhaps we can say there are three tenses, but that they are the present of the past, the present of the present, and the present of the future . . . a triad of the soul . . . recollection . . . observation . . . anticipation." In light of this, our memory of God is most radically encapsulated in celebrating the Eucharistic meal. And this experience profoundly transforms our future. For Augustine, God's presence in our lives reflects his triune being, as Father (memory), Son (understanding) and Spirit (will). These are not three lives but one, so that living in the past is to come near to the beginning, and yet to reach out also to the future. Modern thinking sees memory as a fickle and unreliable guide. But for Augustine, all memory is a process of fabrication, not in the sense of creating fantasy, but in the sense that we mature through reflections on the past—our own and that of the community of believers, past and present. We become habituated by these reflections to act in the light of their assimilation. In memory, we relive.

How tragic that today we think of memorials only in association with death and tombs. In contrast, Mary Carruthers traces the medieval consciousness as replete with memory, "making present the voices of the past, not to entomb either the past or the present, but to give them life together in a place common to both in memory." As Augustine stated, God precedes human memory and indeed every aspect of human thinking, so the first record of our memory should be, "God created me in his image and likeness."

Medieval consciousness was so saturated with this awareness that someone with a great memory was naturally considered a great scholar-saint. When Bernando Gui and Thomas of Celano wrote about the great Thomas Aquinas, this was what they said:

> Of the subtlety and brilliance of his intellect and the soundness of his judgment, sufficient proof is his vast literary output, his many original discoveries, his deep understanding of the Scriptures. His memory was extremely rich and retentive; whatever he once read and grasped he never forgot; it was as if knowledge were ever increasing in his soul as page is added to page in the writing of a book. . . . He never set himself to study or argue a point, or lecture or write and dictate without first having recourse inwardly—but with tears—to prayer for the understanding and the words required by the subject. When perplexed by a difficulty he would kneel and pray, and then, on returning to his writing or dictation, he was accustomed to find that his thought had become so clear that it seemed to show him inwardly, as in a book, the words he needed.

Aquinas's recourse to memory was recourse to God, in dependent prayer. This is how faith continues to be transferred. Our memory of God becomes assimilated by our children and our children's children. It is the memory of loved ones kneeling in prayer.

When all memory has gone, all sense of identity goes also. An individual with no memory is adrift in a present tethered to no past. In our cultural and religious state of amnesia, we have lost all connection to the religious art of the past, the role of the cathedral in the city center, the thousands of biblical references in Dante and Shakespeare, even the dates of the church calendar. But when the Scriptures became critical signposts on our journey, a lamp unto our feet and a light unto our path, then the memory found therein suggests that we can still dwell in community with each other and those who have gone before.

As Augustine puts it, "This is where I bump up against myself, when I call back what I did, and where and when, and how I felt when I was doing it." Likewise, we become both the observer and the observed when we delve into memory. In turn we gain sensitivity to others, learning how to encourage and nurture them as we share from our own memories—for community is built of shared memories. As Augustine notes, "The more by the bond of love we enter into each other's mind, the more even old things become new for us again." Memory is our path to each other, as indeed salvific memory alone is our path to God. It is the memory of the exodus, and indeed of the cross, resurrection and ascension of Christ—indeed, of Pentecost. How glorious, then, is our charge and privilege to transfer this magnificent faith!

Epilogue

Communal Maturity in Christ

√√
Certain authors, speaking of their works, say,
"my book," "my commentary," "my history." . . .
They resemble middle class people who have a house of their own,
and always have "my house" on their tongue.
They would be better to say "our book," "our commentary," "our history"
. . . because there is in them usually more of other people's than their own.

PASCAL
Pensées

The activity of being a writer remains and will always remain,
in the working—out of my life, a secondary function, something faute de mieux.
At its center there is a completely different interest:
the task of renewing the Church.

HANS URS VON BALTHASAR
My Work in Retrospect

. . . Until we all reach unity in the faith and in the knowledge of the Son of God
and become mature, attaining to the whole measure of the fullness of Christ.

EPHESIANS 4:13

Personal convictions are always incomplete. That is why in this book they are collected in only six essays, not seven! It is also why I have chosen the genre of dialectic rather than analysis. For dialogue is social, but to be analytic is a solitary endeavor. We have explored why the personal approach is more effective than conventionality in the transmission of our faith. The personal can penetrate other people's lives as generalizations fail to do. In *The Brothers Karamazov*, Father Zosima tells of frequent visits paid by a stranger in whom Zosima feels "the strongest trust," sensing that "he has some sort of special secret in his soul." The stranger later speaks against the human isolation that prevails over society, so that "everyone now strives most of all to separate his person, wishing to experience the fullness of life within himself, and what comes of all his efforts is not fullness of life but . . . complete isolation." Every now and again someone must break out of the zeitgeist to draw the soul out of its isolation by an act of brotherly communion. For we are not safe in our lonely foxhole; rather, we must seek connection in the whole fabric of the human experience.

Often I have found that what I thought was intimately "me" turns out to be universally "you." Many so-called intimate reflections, such as some of those I have shared in this book, are already in the air around us, universally shared in our common humanity. It is also true that what I assimilate from others becomes so much a part of me that I tend to overlook its source and inspiration in others. So if autobiography is assumed to be a product of the autonomous self, then it is a falsely con-

strued narrative. We should really call it "sociobiography." For as John
Donne reminds us, "No man is an island, entire of itself." Pascal observes
too that any reference to "my book" is false, for the writer has forgotten
how much fruit he has gathered from other minds. Samuel Taylor Coleridge put it more bluntly in his poem *Self-Knowledge*:

> Say, canst thou make thyself?—learn first that trade;—
> Haply thou mayst know what thyself had made.
> What has thou, Man, that thou dar'st call thine own?—
> What is there in thee, Man, that can be known?— . . .
> Vain sister of the worm,—life, death, soul, clod—
> Ignore thyself, and strain to know thy God!

Of course, the apostle Paul had implied long before that Christian
maturity is never the maturity of the individual. Just as God the Father
never acts alone, the Son never acts independently, nor does the Holy
Spirit operate on his own behalf. The Three are One God. Indeed, the
triune God is "with the Other," his being mysteriously linked with creation and humanity as Immanuel, God with us. The biblical God is not
an isolated monad, for he is intrinsically social and love is his being. God
is love and love is of God. Therefore, the Christian life is a corporate reality even though it is a personal experience. Only as we cultivate the
communion of saints can there be any "attaining to the whole measure
of the fullness of Christ" (Eph 4:13).

Perhaps we should consider All Saints' Day, celebrated on November
1, as the most hallowed day of our Christian calendar. It marks the cli-
max of the Christian story, the fulfillment of all the purposes of God that
begin with Epiphany and continue on after Pentecost. This purpose is
most fully expressed in our Lord's high priestly prayer: "That all of them
may be one, Father, just as you are in me and I am in you" (Jn 17:21).
Such union is communion of the body of Christ with the Father, through

the Son, by the Holy Spirit. It is the reality of the truth in love—love manifested, experienced and shared. So the reality of truth is in its experience as love. All true theological education results in community, a community expressive of the triune God of love, flowing naturally out of the state of being open to the mystery of the Trinity.

THE IMPORTANCE OF PERSONAL TRANSMISSION

To some of my readers I may have appeared too severe against professional Christian scholarship and ecclesial ministry. It is essential to exercise rigorous and ethical canons for professional life. But the Christian faith, like other human relationships, more truly belongs to amateurs and dilettantes, lovers who take delight in God. To place faith under a professional microscope and examine it wearing a white lab coat will eventually drive us crazy. There is certainly a place for the college and the clinic, but really, do we need a Ph.D. in motherhood or a master's degree in friendship? What we have subtly been doing in this professional approach to ministry is substituting techniques and technology for love. Even worse, it is the loss of God in daily life that promotes the demand for human expertise. We have become a culture of "experts" because we need authority figures in our lives to replace the divine authority our culture has now denied. Moreover, the erosion of society by the aggressive growth of individualism has introduced "professions" as a new form of tribalism to replace societal values. So, for perhaps many other reasons, we must cling to "experts" today to survive the massive changes in which we are now engulfed. At times this can have amusing consequences. C. S. Lewis put it like this:

> [At school,] when you took the problem to a master, as we all remember, he was very likely to explain what you understood already, to add a great deal of information which you didn't want,

and say nothing at all about the thing that was puzzling you. . . .
The fellow-pupil can help more than the master because he knows
less. The difficulty we want him to explain is the one he has recently
met. The expert met it so long ago that he has forgotten the problem. He sees the whole subject, by now, in such a different light that
he cannot conceive what is really troubling the pupil; he sees a
dozen other difficulties which ought to be troubling him but aren't.

It is a complaint I have often received from students: when they ask
for a cup of cold water, I turn on the fire hydrant! Our tendency to pro-
fessionalize distorts the relational focus of our faith. A friend recently
sent me a wonderful line about this issue. "Jim, remember it was profes-
sionals who built the Titanic, but it was an amateur who built the Ark!"
For professionalism is incapable of handling the mysteries of life—that
is the role of the prophet. As Ivan Illich has pointed out, in the first two
generations of Christianity every community had a prophet. There was
the awareness that something profoundly new had entered into human
history when "the Word became flesh and made his dwelling among us."
So mysterious does the incarnation continue to be that social philosophers such as Charles Taylor find it impossible to explain the contemporary secularization of the Western world without recognizing its profound association with Christianity in the past. We therefore still need
prophets to focus on the mysteries of life and to protest against the
vested interests of the establishment. But we also need them to protest
when the best becomes perverted as the worst, such as is happening with
the gospel when progressively more tools and technology are needed for
it to be effective. *Empowering* is the buzzword we use. As Shakespeare
shrewdly saw,

> For sweetest things turn sourest by their deed;
> Lilies that fester smell far worse than weeds.

I believe that, rather than professional pursuits or even writing meaningful books, the prime action of our lives is the face-to-face encounter with others, bringing God's presence into their lives by being "living epistles," as the apostle puts it. Daily interruptions while working provide a continual reminder that thinking is meaningless without action, indeed that action is meaningless without the cultivation of friendships. But we cannot make a "ministry" out of friendships; it becomes too self-conscious, even manipulative. As Richard Thulin observes, there are three things that are inappropriate in our personal communication: narcissism (a proclamation of self rather than of Christ), privatism (an idiosyncratic reference to self with which the other person can make no connection) and isolationism (a disconnect between the communicator and would-be communicant). The primary aim is to "encourage one another and build each other up" (1 Thess 5:11).

Acting with simplicity helps us gain peace of heart. It is simply dwelling in the presence of God all the time. In turn, a kind spirit will be generous in acknowledging, sharing and cooperating with others as fellow beneficiaries of the grace of God. A test of the genuineness of our "Christian ministry" is how willing we are to share it with others, or indeed to pass it on to others. Monopolizing its agency and making ourselves indispensable is a sure sign that we are in the clutches of professionalism and achievement. My father was fond of reciting the inscription on David Livingstone's tomb in Westminster Abbey: "God lays down his workmen, but he carries on his work."

HAVING A HISTORICAL PERSPECTIVE

It has been said that although we look forward to the future, we learn from the past. This is why the communion of saints is so vital. If we are always living in anticipation of the future, we become ahistorical, capable only of technical-mindedness, eventually becoming morally blind. A firm connection to the past—the early church, the twelfth century, the Reformation, even the nineteenth century—helps us gain deeper perspectives.

In the twelfth century, the era of the reform movement of the early Cistercians, critical changes were taking place: the rise of the individual, the ability of a woman to freely choose her husband, the centrality of friendship and renewed devotion to experiencing the love of God. It was then that the monks rediscovered the role of friendship. Bernard of Clairvaux, his young friend Aelred of Rievaulx and others began to exercise spiritual friendships within monastic culture and were motivated to express God's love at several levels of society. Like Daniel, they encouraged each other in communion with God in the monastery; like Noah, they sought together to save souls in the world; and like Job, they gave spiritual support where the snares of the world were most evident. We may disagree with some of their hierarchical distinctions; nevertheless, they convict us of the high seriousness with which Christians chose to cultivate friendships at that time.

Today no less than then, the search for truth presupposes the growth of *philia*. In such an environment, candles of fresh insight are lit, personalized and shared. The speaker or teacher steps down, unites people in a circle and invites them to share their insights—breaking the bread of truth together. In the morally bland institution, we speak of "my student" or "my parishioner," but as a fiduciary institute, we begin our dialogue as inspired by Aelred: "Here we are, you and I, and, I hope, also a third who is Christ." That is why at the end of life, I do not think in terms of "autobiography," but rather of a life that is richly incremental in many friendships. As Ivan Illich observed, "You can't write the biography of friendship—it's too deeply personal. Friendships run on separate ways that cross and run parallel and cross again."

DIALECTIC THEOLOGY WITH JOHN CALVIN

Some of my Reformed friends may be uncomfortable with the emphasis I give to dialectics. As I argued with my friend Carl Henry years ago, the approach of many evangelicals in the communication of faith has been too emphatically propositional. Yet it is Calvin who is a wise mentor in the use of dialectics. Many would place John Calvin alongside Augustine as one of the greatest fathers of the Western church; both addressed the cultural issues of their day as we now need to do once more. Trained as a lawyer, Calvin gave us the definitive book of Christian doctrine in his *Institutes*, in which he exercises his trusteeship of faith and critiques religious institutions with remarkable theological insights. This he does at the turning point between the medieval and the modern worlds.

We can nominate Calvin as that one person who, as Father Zosima described, courageously broke through his culture to be a witness to the truth of God in a changing world. Medieval scholasticism's cozy confidence in a Ptolemaic universe where all the planets revolved around the earth was being shattered by knowledge of an expanding heliocentric universe and the discovery of the New World. It became fashionable in the sixteenth century and after to systematize knowledge, separating it into divisions and subdivisions according to the educational concepts of Pierre Ramus. He reduced rhetoric to mere technique and allocated invention, argument and arrangement to philosophy. Reason was split from ethics, and since then ethics has been attached only precariously to theology. Calvin, who preceded Ramus, detested systematization and abstract speculation, concluding that human reason can never grasp the gospel, nor can it reduce the Christian life to analytic and encyclopedic thought. Rather than inductive analysis, participatory knowledge is how humans discover God's divine being as Immanuel, God with us.

This mystery of participation lies at the heart of faith. Christ's role as

our mediator is due to his nature within the triune God, but it doesn't
end with us, according to Calvin. Christ reconciles us to the Father because of sin, but as co-Creator he also mediates everything in creation.
Likewise, Calvin viewed the Holy Spirit as the agent of participation, for
"by means of him we come to participate in God." Calvin clearly separates Creator and creature in order to relate them properly in gracious
participation. Sin does separate us from God, but it does not overcome
God's own being as Immanuel. Calvin affirms the transcendence of God
against the abuse of cozy medieval pietism, but he also states, "The
proper condition of creatures is to keep close to God." His emphasis on
transcendence is to establish the freedom of God to choose a life of communion with his creature. Hence divine transcendence does not imply
distance but a basis for true intimacy.

Likewise, Christ is the firstborn, not in chronology but relationally as
the Son of God. With such a revolutionary shift from Aristotelian essence
to relational being, Calvin interpreted the nature of humanity not in
terms of substance, but rather in terms of relationality. He thus developed a "theological anthropology," maintaining that it is God who defines our humanity, not some natural cause. Calvin therefore implacably
resisted the incipient popular usage of "nature" as a substantial category
of its own. Nature was a relational reality: it was either in communion
with God, or else it was alienated from God. He was already teaching this
in his early Christian work.

In this regard, Calvin was following the Christian humanist tradition
of the Renaissance, which saw doctrine as confessional, not doctrinaire,
for its purpose lies in seeking communion with God. As Dante's contemporary Petrarch affirmed, "What is the use of knowing what virtue is, if
it is not loved when known? What is the use of knowing sin, if it is not
abhorred when known?" Yet Calvin went further than Augustine in his
trinitarian theology, since late medieval Nominalism had divided God's

being in himself from God's action in the history of salvation. Calvin affirmed with the Cappadocian fathers, rather than with the Latin fathers, that the triune God does not have an impersonal "divine essence," but by mutual coinherence and the interpersonal life of fellowship between the Father, Son and Holy Spirit, God reaches out to us in redemptive communion.

Thus Calvin did not have a "system" of theology, for the incarnation and ascension were his paradigm. The union of the deity and the humanity of Jesus Christ generated two ways of looking at God, which Calvin grounded in the formula *distincto sed non separatio*, distinct but not separate. These two movements—the down-stooping of God in Christ and the upraising of the dignity of man in Jesus—are both expressed in the divine revelation that Calvin celebrated. They are still the basis for Christian paradox today, as we have explored in these essays. Our faith is concave and convex, downward yet upward, inverse and converse (as sinners we need to invert our attitudes in order to be converted). Moreover, God and the world and God and man cannot be divorced from the other. There is time and there is also eternity—the eternal God came in the fullness of time. There is God's foreknowledge yet there is human freedom. There is the provisional nature of our earthly life, yet there is our sure and certain hope of heaven.

IN SEASON AND OUT OF SEASON

We began this book by observing that the cultural tsunami of secular humanism is sweeping over our whole world, threatening to carry away all traditional landmarks of Christianity. The apostle Paul on Mars Hill in Athens had more in common with the pagan philosophers, the Stoics and Epicureans with whom he debated, than we have today with this secular psyche. The sense of the self was much more porous then, more open to the divine, to metanarratives and metaphysics, than the insulated and impermeable technical self is today. What then of Paul's injunction to Timothy to "be prepared in season and out of season" (2 Tim 4:2)? Perhaps our response should be multilayered. As Paul tells the Philippians, "I have learned the secret of being content in any and every situation" (Phil 4:11-12).

When our ultimate contentment is in God alone, we remain unmoved by changing and contradictory circumstances. Sir Thomas More has been admired as a man for all seasons. Early in his life he desired to become a Carthusian monk, to live a solitary, silent life. Instead, his brilliance made him tutor to the royal prince and eventually chancellor of England, second only to the king. But for all those years, unbeknownst even to his wife, he wore a hair shirt beneath his courtier's garments and robes to remind himself of his primary identity as a forgiven sinner. When his friend and former pupil Henry VIII turned against him and condemned him to death, his last words were, "I die the king's servant, but God's first." One of his gifts to the church was a small devotional book called *The Last Things,* which reminds us that death, judgment, hell and heaven should always be on our minds and in our ears. On the scaffold he quoted Paul's words in Philippians 3:8: "I consider everything a loss compared to the surpassing greatness of knowing Christ Jesus my Lord, for whose sake I have lost all things. I consider them rubbish, that I may gain Christ."

But does the apostle leave us with being "in season and out of season"? No, for he is not using the term *chronos,* or temporal time, but *kairos,* the eventfulness of God's intervention in time. For the Christian, the seasons of life are not determined by the calendar, nor by climatic seasons, nor even by the psychological stages between birth and death; they are God's seasons in our life. God moves in and out, in consolation as well as in apparent withdrawal, to comfort and to afflict, teaching us that the vicissitudes of life are instruments he uses in relating to us. The outcome is that we are more blessed in suffering than we would be in a bland and superficial existence. This, of course, is what we witness in the Psalms, where the flow of the psalmist's experiences encompasses all the range and exigencies of human emotion. And it is Christ's love that "binds them all together in perfect unity" (Col 3:14).

The French poet Charles Peguy has pointed out that the least harmful interpretation of reality has been the materialist view. It is naive enough to deny the eternal and so reduce everything to the temporal. But as these essays display, far more dangerous is the religious "pie in the sky" approach that denies the temporal in advocacy of the eternal. This too is motivated by self-expediency: in professing the eternal we can live without sacrifice. It lets us conform to common sense rather than acknowledging the mystery that seeks to live the temporal life in the light of the eternal. Openness to God has profound temporal consequences if we truly and consistently answer our call as Christians.

Such then are some of the convictions that have brought me to live dangerously on the edge yet joyously in exile. We start Christian service thinking that our natural interests and abilities can combine with God's grace to achieve a noble cause. Then God begins to prune our lives, and we are ready to run away. But in the end the humble see God's love in the smallest of things, whereas the proud don't recognize the hand of God in the greatest of events. The advice of my favorite poet, George Herbert, is that it is better to remain in loyal and humble service to the king of love.

When first thou didst entice to thee my heart
I thought the service brave:
So many joys I writ down for my part,
Besides what I might have
Out of my stock of natural delights,
Augmented with thy gracious benefits. . . .

Whereas my birth and spirit rather took
The way that takes the town;
Thou didst betray me to a lingering book,
And wrap me in a gown.
I was entangled in the world of strife,
Before I had the power to change my life. . . .

Yet, though thou troublest me, I must be meek;
In weakness must be stout.
Well, I will change the service, and go seek
Some other master out.
Ah, my dear God! though I am clean forget,
Let me not love, if I love thee not.

Appendix

Why the Rhetoric of Dialectics?

Throughout the history of the church, confusion has existed between the role of dogma and the abuse of dogmatism. *Dogma* refers to an authoritative tenet of faith, and hence to the body of doctrines that comprise the core of the Christian faith. But *dogmatism* refers to the attitude we hold regarding these basic convictions. We should be decisive in holding our convictions, but the excess of this decisiveness often manifests itself in rigidity or even arrogance, thus becoming "dogmatism." This usually results in inadequate examination of the vitality and fullness of the truth of our convictions, and we instead become doctrinaire and authoritarian. In contrast, the appropriate way to express dogma is to do so confidently and yet humbly, being modest in one's own understanding and yet being transformed by one's convictions. This is why dialectics are appropriate to the communication of dogma. For by discussion and reasoning together, the truth is communicated personally—literally, in conversation together (Greek *dialektikos,* "of conversation").

THE ORIGINAL ROLE OF DIALECTICS IN TRUTHFUL PERSUASION

Plato used Socrates as a dialectician to help clear away the accumulated false persuasions of the Sophists who were more concerned with appearance and rhetorical techniques than the serious quest for truth. So rhetoric became abused to the point of being little more than manipulation, or what today we would call "brainwashing." But Socrates, by asking the right questions, removed the dross accumulated by his own conventional culture to rediscover the gold nuggets of truth. So we are likewise asking in these essays, is the evangelical culture producing "brainwashed Gnostic Christians"? This may lead to knowledgeable "beliefs," but do they give life in being "truthful"? For the essence of true persuasion has always been based upon the moral character (ethos) of the rhetor, not merely upon his skill in rhetoric.

We cannot dismiss the role of rhetoric, for our Christian witness demands the appropriate art of persuasion. Dialectics help us reflect on the intrinsic difficulty of being a Christian, as being in this world but not of it. Reflection on the application of Christian thought to Christian living must be basic to our faith. What is merely doctrinaire, descriptive and prescriptive is not enough, though this emphasis has a legacy from the sixteenth century when the memorization of the catechism was adopted as a great tool of the Reformation. From its onset, entering into "the modern world" of the new discoveries of the Americas, Protestant thought became saturated by inductive thinking to create dictionaries, directories, classifications, definitions, etc. These have left us the legacy of "systematic theology," in which there tends to be a dualism between thought and action.

Added to this, after the thirteenth century no longer did a Christian scholar need to qualify also as a saint, as the early fathers all exemplified. The split between sanctity and scholarship has intensified since then to the detriment of "holy living." That is why so much contemporary theological scholarship is no more than journalism about theological issues. As Martin Luther commented on the lament for the loss of truth expressed in Psalm 12, "None of you can pray a psalm if you have not previously made the words of the psalm your own. But they will then be your own when you have the same feeling and the same spirit in which the words were said." Crying out in the actual experience of a shipwreck is not the same as using the same words on the stage to reenact a shipwreck as a theatrical drama. So dialectics can express protest against pseudo-reality and disembodied religious talk.

THE ROLE OF DIALECTICS IN PERSONALIZING KNOWLEDGE

Even within secular culture today there is a growing disenchantment with the rationalism of modernity. This opens up a fresh opportunity to revive serious Christian reflection on conventional Christian morality. So we find ourselves entering once more into a more personal dialogue between God's Word and our mutual responses. For the subjunctive mood given us by Rene Descartes—"I think therefore I am"—now needs the corrective of the indicative mood—"Thus says the Lord"—to recover a deeper, living biblical faith, whether we are Protestant, Roman Catholic or Orthodox in affiliation.

For behind the basic issues of our Christian faith, we are living with the dialectic between speculative thought and human existence, between reason and faith, between the "poetic" and the "prudent," between the "personal fiduciary institute" and the more irresponsible "public institution," and indeed, between the temporal and the eternal. These are different spheres of our humanity where we need to make distinctions and establish boundaries to "social thought," while engaging within "personal reality." For the illusion of being a "thinker" is that it assumes thought and existence are united, when of course "thought" can merely be "daydreaming" about existence. Every theological student is in fact aware that such cognitive studies often drive one away from the daily practice of a devotional Christian life. Actually, the abstraction of "thought" indicates that one is not paying enough attention to oneself as a "person" in the process of merely being a "thinker." That is to say, it lacks the ethical dimension of being socially related and responsible to

others. For to "exist in truth" implies being both truthful to one's self and
also to others, thus considerably enhancing the meaning of "existence."
To then think and exist personally "before God" vastly expands both the
breadth of thought and the depth of our existence.

KIERKEGAARD'S USE OF INVERSE DIALECTICS
FOR TRANSFORMATION

Søren Kierkegaard, as a Christian "Socrates," identified the nineteenth
century as culturally the most fraudulent in the history of Christianity.
Perhaps he would see our century as even worse. So, he argues, Christians need to challenge and confront the culture dialectically. But the
Danish word for dialectics, *Gjentagelse,* is more expressive than our English term, for it speaks of a situation that is "the same" (*Gjen* means "already in existence") but is now being reinterpreted in an original way as
"the other" (*at tage* refers to "a new reality, truly new"). In his short meditation on this term (1843), Kierkegaard speaks of dialectics as being a
new creative synthesis of uniting opposites. He acknowledges that Socrates possessed "the idea of dialectic," knowing that the eternal is, but
not what or who the eternal is. So Socrates could distinguish between
what is qualitative and what is quantitative. Kierkegaard certainly em-
phasized the qualitative as existential, so he saw that existential dialectic
comes to expression when a human being recognizes the qualitative contradiction between one's present condition and one's existential telos. In
the exercise of dialectic, one denies a negative to replace it with a greater
positive. But the Christian is most keenly aware of human incongruities
that challenge incapacities by potentially greater capacities, such as the
bondage of sin overcome by grace, death overcome by resurrection,
mortality giving place to the eternal. For Kierkegaard the importance of
irony is its role as negative used to open our eyes to a greater view of human existence. Yet unlike Hegel's use of dialectic where the negative is

the producer of a higher positive of *thought,* Kierkegaard seeks for a deeper positivity of the ethical beyond just *thought* about the good.

This is why Kierkegaard speaks of "inverse dialectics" as the form taken by the existential dialectic in the sphere of the ethical. As sinners we need to live in constant denial of a self-centered life, so that the negative becomes a permanent constant. It is the Pauline way of life: "I live, yet not I, but Christ lives in me" (Gal 2:20, modified KJV). It is what Kierkegaard's literary character Climaticus calls "dying away to immediacy," which belongs to the sufferings of "hidden inwardness" because it implies the transformation of our existence in relation to God. It is the consciousness of guilt, impotence and distance from God to embrace the eternal in its revelation of "Jesus Christ and him crucified" (1 Cor 2:2). True religion or, as he calls it, "Religion B," is seeing the potentiality of one's life not within one's self but only in Jesus Christ and the indwelling of the Holy Spirit. So the inverse dialectic of the Christian life is seeing the positive role played by suffering, sacrifice and self-giving, which helps clarify the essential values of being a Christian.

Thus the Christian has bifocal vision in seeing exaltation in humiliation, strength in weakness, Christlikeness in selflessness. Christian inverse dialectics actually work against self-interest. Moreover, the Christian does not strive directly for the eternal, but indirectly and inversely. Its values are existential and relational—reconciliation, forgiveness, new life, faith, hope, love, joy, peace. Yet the Christian life poses constant offense by colliding against the status quo and the established order of worldly values, as well by the constitutive "sign of offense" that the centrality of the cross of Christ inevitably brings into the world. Moreover the consciousness of sin is never far from the true Christian, and the constant dying away from the world becomes one's way of life. Thus the more truth one seeks to live, the more opposition one will encounter.

Notes

Prologue: Why Dialectics?

Page 19 "Our starting point": Karl Barth, *Church Dogmatics* 3/4, trans. G. W. Bromiley and T. F. Torrance (Edinburgh: T & T Clark, 1961), p. 376.

Page 21 Jacques Ellul's book: Jacques Ellul, *The Presence of the Kingdom*, trans. Olive Wyon, 2nd ed. (Colorado Springs: Helmer & Howard, 1989).

Page 22 "He never could distinguish": H. R. Mackintosh, *Types of Modern Theology* (London: Fontana Library, 1964), p. 141.

Page 22 It was easy for nominal Christians: Walter E. Houghton, *The Victorian Frame of Mind, 1830-1870* (New Haven, Conn.: Yale University Press, 1985), pp. 305-339.

Page 24 "Belsen, Hiroshima and Dachau": William Golding, *A Moving Target* (London: Faber & Faber, 1965), p. 102.

Page 24 Perhaps he was describing: Randall Stevenson, *The Last of England?*, The Oxford English Literary History (Oxford: Oxford University Press, 2004), 12:508.

Page 25 Artistic expression "alone possesses": Werner Jaeger, *The Ideals of Greek Culture,* trans. Gilbert Highet, 2nd ed. (Oxford: Oxford University Press, 1965), 1:36-37.

Page 26 "A book must be the axe": Quoted by Alberto Manguel, *A History of Reading* (Toronto: Vintage Books, 1998), p. 93.

Page 26 "You cannot embark on life": Orhan Pamuk, *The White Castle,* quoted by Manguel, p. 23.

Page 27 "I will force [the Russian socialists]": *Selected Letters of Fyodor Dostoyevsky*, ed. Joseph Frank and David I. Goldstein, trans. Andrew R. MacAndrew (New Brunswick, N.J.: Rutgers University Press, 1987) pp. 469-70.

1 The Breath of the Hidden Life

Page 34   "To a Christian": W. H. Auden, *The Dyer's Hand and Other Essays* (New York: Random House, 1962), p. 457.

Page 34   "It is impossible": Ibid.

Page 41   "Observance, discipline, thought": T. S. Eliot, "The Dry Salvages."

Page 43   The toxic disease: Richard Rohr, *Everything Belongs: The Gift of Contemplative Prayer* (New York: Crossroads, 1999), p. 18.

Page 46   "When death is": Søren Kierkegaard, *Sickness unto Death,* taken from *The Essential Kierkegaard,* ed. Howard V. Hong and Edna H. Hong (Princeton, N.J.: Princeton University Press, 1978-2000), 11:148, 151, 213.

Page 46   Without Christian earnestness: Robert Widenman, "Christian Earnestness," in *The Sources and Depths of Faith in Kierkegaard,* Bibliotheca Kierkegaardiana, ed. Niels Thulstup and Marie Mikulova Thulstrup (Copenhagen: C. A. Reitzels Boghandel, 1978), p. 83.

Page 48   Neurotic drives and passions: Erich Kahler, *The Tower and the Abyss* (New York: George Braziller, 1959), p. 165.

Page 48   What Edgar Allen Poe had called: Robert L. Belknap, "Dostoevskii and Psychology," in W. J. Leatherbarrow, *The Cambridge Companion to Dostoevskii* (Cambridge: Cambridge University Press, 2002), p. 136.

Page 49   "He is as selfish": René Girard, *Resurrection from the Underground* (New York: Crossroad, 1997), pp. 147-51.

Page 49   "Little Cartesian gods": Ibid., p. 155.

2 Being Open to a Visionary Life Before God

Page 53   Pascal found that: Blaise Pascal, *Pensées* in *The Mind on Fire,* ed. James M. Houston, Victor Classics (Colorado Springs: Cook, 2006), p. 44.

Page 55   "You are right": Quotations are from Belinda Thomson, *Vision of the Sermon: The Story Behind the Painting* (Edinburgh: National Galleries of Scotland, 2005), p. 5.

Page 57   "He recollected God": Quoted by Michael Watts, *Kierkegaard* (Oxford: Oneworld, 2003), p. 206.

Page 57   "When death": Søren Kierkegaard, *Sickness unto Death*, taken from *The Essential Kierkegaard,* ed. Howard V. Hong and Edna H. Hong (Princeton, N.J.: Princeton University Press, 1978-2000), p. 132.

Page 59   "The matter of getting rid": William Anz, "Kierkegaard on Death and Dying," in *Kierkegaard: A Critical Reader,* ed. Jonathan Ree and Jane Chamberlain (Oxford: Blackwell, 1998), p. 39.

Page 60   From that point on: See the focus on the ascension given freshly by
              Douglas Farrow, *Ascension and Ecclesia* (Grand Rapids: Eerdmans,
              1999).

Page 61   "Effective leadership": Ray S. Anderson, *The Soul in Ministry* (Louis-
              ville, Ky.: John Knox Press, 1997), p. 199.

Page 61   "Our minds go into a spin": Gregory of Nazianzus, *Second Theological
              Oration* 31.

Page 61   Yet angels form: Lou H. Silberman, "Prophets/Angels: LXX and Qum-
              ran Psalm 151 and the Epistle to the Hebrews," in *Standing Before God:
              Essays in Honor of John M. Oesterreicher*, ed. Asher Finkel and Lawrence
              Frizzell (New York: Knav, 1981), pp. 91-101.

Page 62   In Exodus: See George E. Mendenhall, *Ancient Israel's Faith and History*,
              ed. Gary A. Herion (Louisville, Ky.: John Knox Press, 2001), pp. 206-7.

Page 64   Serious theological objections: Karl Barth, *Church Dogmatics* 3/4, trans.
              Geoffrey W. Bromiley and T. F. Torrance (Edinburgh: T & T Clark,
              1961), p. 59; Ibid. 4/4, p. 11.

Page 64   Does mystical experience: Ibid. 1/2, pp. 319-20.

Page 65   For John of the Cross: David Knowles, *The English Mystical Tradition*
              (New York: Harper Torchbooks, 1965).

Page 65   "Rare occurrences": John of the Cross, *The Living Flame* 1.15.2.

Page 66   "Words strain": T. S. Eliot, "Burnt Norton," lines 149-53.

Page 66   Modern culture: Colin P. Thompson, *The Poet and the Mystic: A Study
              of the Cantico Espiritual of San Juan de la Cruz* (Oxford: Oxford Univer-
              sity Press, 1977), p. 146.

Page 66   Neurophysiologists tell us: Antonio Demasio, *The Feeling of What Hap-
              pened* (New York: Harcourt, Brace, 1999), pp. 195-200.

Page 66   "I am certain": Barbara Reynolds, *The Letters of Dorothy L. Sayers* (New
              York: St. Martin's, 1998), 2:213.

Page 66   Augustine speaks: Garry Wells, *Saint Augustine's Memory* (New York:
              Viking, 2002).

Page 67   "A pronounced openness": Klaus Berger, *Identity and Experience in the
              New Testament*, trans. Charles Muenchow (Minneapolis: Fortress,
              2003), p. 12.

Page 69   "Faith is one's": Ibid., p. 106.

Page 69   His meditative study: Jean Vanier, *Drawn into the Mystery of Jesus
              through the Gospel of John* (New York: Paulist, 2004), p. 13.

Page 69   In him we do not: Ibid., p. 13.

Page 70   "We need no barbarous": Quoted from "Spirits in Bondage" by Corbin Scott Carnell, *Bright Shadow of Reality: Spiritual Longing in C. S. Lewis* (Grand Rapids: Eerdmans, 1999), p. 117.

Page 71   "If the heavens": T. F. Torrance, "The Spiritual Relevance of Angels" in *Alive to God: Studies in Spirituality*, ed. J. I. Packer and Loren Wilkinson (Downers Grove, Ill.: InterVarsity Press, 1992), p. 126.

Page 73   "Ye holy angels": *Church Hymnal*, 3rd ed. (Oxford: Oxford University Press, 1973), no. 363.

Pages 74-75   "It happened this way": Jerry Levin, *Reflections on My First Noel* (Birmingham: Hope Publishing House, 2002), p. 24.

Page 79   She remained fully: See the stimulating article by Birgit Bertung, "Yes, a Woman Can Exist," in *Kierkegaard, Poet of Existence*, ed. Birgit Bertung (Copenhagen: C.A. Reitzel, 1989), pp. 7-18.

3 The Surrealism of Christian Public Life

Page 84   "It is an astonishing thing": Pascal *Pensées*, 434, Brunschweig.

Page 88   "Not being diverted": *Stromateis* 3.97.2.

Page 88   "The Puritans first recognized": See John Morgan, *Godly Learning: towards Reason, Learning and Education, 1560-1640* (Cambridge: Cambridge University Press, 1986).

Page 89   The "genius" and the "apostle": Søren Kierkegaard, *On Authority and Revelation: The Book of Adler* (Princeton, N.J.: Princeton University Press, 1941).

Page 89   "Any genuine 'apostle'": W. H. Auden, *The Dyer's Hand and Other Essays* (New York: Random House, 1962), p. 443.

Page 93   "No one hears": John G. Stackhouse, ed. *Evangelical Ecclesiology: Reality or Illusion?* (Grand Rapids: Baker, 2003), p. 214.

Page 94   We have created: Albert Borgmann, *Power Failure* (Grand Rapids: Brazos, 2003), pp. 28-29.

Page 95   "The shining ones": John Betjeman, "Christmas," in *The Faber Book of Religious Verse*, ed. Helen Gardner (London: Faber and Faber, 1972), p. 329.

Page 96   The Peace of Westphalia: Bruce Hindmarsh, "Is Evangelical Ecclesiology an Oxymoron?" in *Evangelical Ecclesiology*, pp. 15-37.

Page 96   It commenced with: Peter Brown, *The Rise of Western Christendom* (Oxford: Blackwell, 2003), pp. 60-64.

Page 96   "Christ himself abolished": Malcolm Muggeridge, *The End of Christendom* (Grand Rapids: Eerdmans, 1980), p. 14.

Page 97   "The reality of Christ": Ibid., p. 62.

Page 98   Most people took refuge: Jorgen Bukdahl, *Søren Kierkegaard and the Common Man*, trans., rev., ed. Bruce H. Kirmmse (Grand Rapids: Eerdmans, 2001), p. 3.

Page 98   Was it necessary: In the Danish newspaper *Faedrelandet* ("The Father Fatherland"), December 27, 1854, p. 97.

Page 98   "Preach Christianity fast": Søren Kierkegaard, *Journals and Papers,* ed. and trans. Howard V. Hong and Edna H. Hong (Bloomington: Indiana University Press, 1967-1978), 1:329.

Page 98   "In an impermissible": *Training in Christianity*, p. 38.

Page 98   "The absolute contemporary": Ibid., pp. 66-68.

Page 99   It makes faith so vivid: Ibid., p. 236.

Page 99   Anyone who depicts: Ibid., p. 210.

Page 99   But we only live: Ibid., p. 105.

Page 100   "Man is a fallen being": Randall Stevenson, *The Last of England* (Oxford: Oxford University Press, 2004), p. 417.

Page 100   Envy is actually: Rene Girard, *The Girard Reader,* ed. James G. Williams, (New York: Crossroad, 1996), p. 289.

Page 101   "I thought I was chosen": William Golding, *The Spire* (London: Faber and Faber, 1964), p. 25.

Page 101   "I thought I was doing": Ibid., p. 168.

Page 102   "What is faith?": Ibid., p. 190.

Page 102   "Consent, and no sin": Ibid., p. 178.

Page 102   "Naggingly conscious": Saul Bellow, "The Writer as Moralist," *Atlantic Monthly,* March 1963, p. 61.

Page 103   "There is no innocent work": Golding, *The Spire*, p. 222.

4 The Journey Toward Becoming a Person

Page 104   "The process whereby": Duncan MacLaren, *Mission Implausible: Restoring Credibility to the Church* (London: Paternoster, 2005), p. 89.

Page 107   A view of the idea of the "person": Lucian Turcescu, "'Person' versus 'Individual,' and Other Misreadings of Gregory of Nyssa," *Modern Theology* 18, no. 4 (2002): 527-39.

Page 109 "The reality and the relevance": James Houston, "A God-Centered Personality," in *Why I Am Still a Christian*, ed. E. M. Blaiklock (Grand Rapids: Eerdmans, 1971), p. 83.

Page 109 "The isolated purely": John Macmurray, *The Self as Agent* (London: Faber, 1957), p. 38.

Page 110 His writings later: Philip Conford, *The Personal World: John Macmurray on Self and Society* (Edinburgh: Floris Books, 1996).

Page 110 The Gifford Lectures: Macmurray, *Self as Agent*.

Page 111 They rejected its three: Isaiah Berlin, *The Roots of Romanticism* (Princeton, N.J.: Princeton University Press, 1999), pp. 21-22.

Page 111 Technology produces: Erich Kahler, *The Tower and the Abyss: An Inquiry into the Transformation of the Individual* (New York: George Brazilier, 1957), pp. 91-97.

Page 111 Addressing loneliness: J. H. van den Berg, *A Different Existence* (Pittsburgh: Duquesne University Press, 1972), pp. 105-106.

Page 111 Loneliness is the result: Richard Stivers, *Shades of Loneliness: Pathologies of a Technological Society* (Lanham, Md.: Rowman and Littlefield, 2004), p. 55.

Page 112 "The lonely crowd": David Riesman, *The Lonely Crowd* (Garden City, N.Y.: Doubleday, 1953).

Page 112 A poisonous atmosphere: Peter J. Frost, *Toxic Emotions at Work: How Compassionate Managers Handle Pain and Conflict* (Boston: Harvard Business School Press, 2004).

Page 113 Suddenly, he appreciated: Ibid., p. 130.

Page 113 The fireside has: It is ironic that the use of two pervasive technical terms today, from the Greek *technē* and *oikos*, were first applied to Christian family life. "Technomatria" was first used by the Puritans in the 1590s to refer to the governance of the home in a godly manner, while "domestic economy" meant the management of family devotions, such as daily family prayers and Bible reading. It was only at the end of the eighteenth century that "the management of nations" was used by Adam Smith for economic affairs; "technology" had an even later origin.

Page 114 Our heat no longer: Albert Borgmann, *Power Failure* (Grand Rapids, Mich.: Brazos, 2003).

Page 115 His pioneering book: Leonard Hodgson, *The Doctrine of the Trinity*

(London: Nisbet, 1943).

Page 115   He has been as influential: Colin E. Gunton, *The Promise of Trinitarian Theology* (Edinburgh: T & T Clark, 1991).

Page 115   Greek theologian: John D. Zizioulas, *Being as Communion* (London: Darton, Longman and Todd, 1985).

Page 117   Journey into personhood: A helpful introduction is Joseph Gallagher, *To Hell and Back with Dante: A Modern Reader's Guide to the Divine Comedy* (Liguori, Mo.: Triumph, 1996).

Page 118   Behind all of these: Giuseppe di Scipio, *The Presence of Pauline Thought in the Works of Dante: Studies in Art and Religious Interpretation* (Lewiston, N.Y.: Edwin Mellen, 1995).

Page 119   Human desire is insatiable: A suggestive guide for the contemporary application of *The Divine Comedy* is Alan Jones, *The Soul's Journey: Exploring the Spiritual Life with Dante as Guide* (Cambridge, Mass.: Cowley, 2001).

Page 122   "O you who are of sound": Quoted by Giuseppe Mazzotta, *Dante, Poet of the Desert: History and Allegory in the Divine Comedy* (Princeton, N.J.: Princeton University Press, 1979), p. 277.

5 Living the Truth in Love

Page 128   Bologna was full: Harriet Rubin, *Dante in Love* (New York: Simon & Schuster, 2004), p. 209.

Page 132   The seventy-year exile: See Peter R. Ackroyd, *Exile and Restoration* (Philadelphia: Westminster Press, 1968), pp. 240-41.

Page 133   The claim that we belong: Brian S. Rosner, *Paul, Scripture & Ethics* (Grand Rapids: Baker, 1994), pp. 123-36.

Page 133   Indicts evangelical culture: Mark Strom, *Reframing Paul: Conversations in Grace and Community* (Downers Grove, Ill.: InterVarsity Press, 2000), pp. 13-17, 201-43.

Page 133   A misunderstanding among: Andre Resner Jr., *Preacher and Cross* (Grand Rapids: Eerdmans, 1999), p. 6.

Page 134   "Lord, how can man": George Herbert, *The Country Parson, The Temple,* Classics of Western Spirituality, (Mahweh, N.J.: Paulist, 1981), pp. 183-84.

Page 137   Anyone reading his works: An excellent guide to Bunyan's literary methods is described in U. M. Kaufmann, *The Pilgrim's Progress and*

Tradition in Puritan Meditation (New Haven, Conn.: Yale University Press, 1966).

Page 139   Bunyan, himself a nonconformist: For a careful theological interpretation of his book, see Richard L. Greaves, *John Bunyan* (Grand Rapids: Eerdmans, 1969).

Page 139   "I know of no Book": Quoted by Monica Furlong, *Pilgrim's Progress* (New York: Coward, McCann & Geoghegan, 1975), p. 183.

Page 141   "A future finer": U. Milo Kaufman, *Heaven: A Future Finer than Dreams* (Indianapolis: Light & Life Communications, 1981), p. 25.

Page 141   "[The hero Ransom] had read of 'Space'": C. S. Lewis, *Out of the Silent Planet* (New York: Collier, 1965), p. 32.

Page 142   "If we could even effect": Ibid., p. 154.

Page 142   Evangelical scholars sometimes: Allen C. Guelzo, "Piety and Intellect: America's theologian," *Christian Century*, October 4, 2003, p. 30.

Page 143   "True virtue never": Jonathan Edwards, "A Treatise Concerning Religious Affections," *Works*, ed. John E. Smith (New Haven, Conn.: Yale University Press, 1959), 2:93, 95.

Page 143   Self-deception works: Ava Chamberlain, "Self-Deception as a Theological Problem in Jonathan Edwards's 'Treatise Concerning Religious Affections,'" *Church History* 63, no. 4, 1994, pp. 541-56.

Page 143   "Gracious affections have": Edwards, *Works*, p. 253.

Page 143   "Sanctifies the reason": Ibid., pp. 307-8.

Page 144   "Then the more": Ibid., p. 377.

Page 144   "To speak of Christian experience": Ibid., pp. 450-51.

Page 144   "For someone who was": George M. Marsden, *Jonathan Edwards: A Life* (New Haven, Conn.: Yale University Press, 2003), p. 374.

Page 145   "Edwards challenges": Ibid., p. 503.

Page 145   Frequent Saturday evening discussions: James M. Houston, "Reminiscences of the Oxford Lewis," in *We Remember C. S. Lewis*, ed. David Graham (Nashville: Broadman & Holman, 2001), pp. 129-143.

Page 146   "He replied that": James M. Houston, "C. S. Lewis's Concern for the Future of Humanity," *Knowing and Doing, Quarterly Journal of the C. S. Lewis Institute,* spring 2006: 8-9, 22-24.

Page 146   "The good catastrophe": J. R. R. Tolkien, "On Fairy Stories," in *Essays Presented to Charles Williams*, ed. C. S. Lewis (Grand Rapids: Eerdmans, 1966), p. 81.

Page 146   "The imagination, then": Colin Duriez, "The Romantic Writer: Lewis's
            Theology of Fantasy," in C. S. Lewis, *The Pilgrim's Guide: C. S. Lewis and
            the Art of the Witness*, ed. David Mills (Grand Rapids: Eerdmans, 1998),
            p. 103.

Page 147   The classic myth: C. S. Lewis, *Till We Have Faces: A Myth Retold* (Grand
            Rapids: Eerdmans, 1966).

6 Christian Transmission in an Age of Disjunction

Page 150   It is authoritative: See the essays of Robert L. Wilken, *Remembering the
            Christian Past* (Grand Rapids: Eerdmans, 2003), p. 174.

Page 150   "The faithful departed": Robert Louis Wilken, *The Spirit of Early Chris-
            tian Thought* (New Haven, Conn.: Yale University Press, 2003), p. 47.

Page 153   "Friendship brings": Nicholas Zernov, *Sunset Years: A Russian Pilgrim in
            the West* (London: Fellowship of St. Alban & St. Sergius, 1983), p. 123.

Page 154   "Standing on the edge": Nicholas Zernov, *Three Russian Prophets* (Lon-
            don: S.C.M. Press, 1944), p. 84.

Page 154   "Dostoyevsky is both": Diane Oenning Thompson, *The Brothers Kara-
            mazov and the Poetics of Memory* (Cambridge: Cambridge University
            Press, 1992), p. 226.

Page 155   "There is nothing": Joseph Frank and David I. Goldstein, eds., *Selected
            Letters of Fyodor Dostoevsky*, trans. Andrew H. MacAndrew (New Bruns-
            wick, N.J.: Rutgers University Press, 1987).

Page 155   "If only I could depict": Quoted by Nadeja Gorodetzky, *Saint Tikhon of
            Zadonsk* (Crestwood, N.Y.: St. Vladimir's Seminary Press, 1976), p.
            223-24.

Page 156   "A first [Russian] attempt": Ibid., p. 235.

Page 156   He begged adults: Ibid., p. 127.

Page 156   "Much on earth": Fyodor Dostoyevsky, *The Brothers Karamazov*, trans.
            Robert Pevear and Larissa Volokhonsky (San Francisco: North Point,
            1990), p. 320.

Page 157   "The dogma which expresses": Vladimir Lossky, *The Mystical Theology
            of the Eastern Church* (Crestwood, N.Y.: St Vladimir's Seminary Press,
            1976), p. 10.

Page 158   Instead a new model: G. Davies, "Believing Without Belonging: Is This
            the Future of Religion in Britain?" *Social Compass* 37 (1990): 456-69.

Page 158   Catholic sociologists: See, for example, Juan Martin Velasco, ed., *Trans-*

mision de la Fe en la Sociedad Actual: Instituto Superior de Pastoral (Salamanca: University of Salamanca Press, Editorial Verbo Divino, 1991).

Page 158   A French Catholic writer: J.-M. R. Tillard, *Sommes-Nous les Derniers Chrétiens?* (Paris: Fides, 1997).

Page 159   "Each of us has one Master": Augustine *De Magistro*; also *Sermo* 134.1; 38.72.

Page 160   A group of educational philosophers: Alan M. Olson, David M. Steiner and Anna S. Tuuli, *Educating for Democracy: Paideia in an Age of Uncertainty* (Lanham, Md.: Rowman & Littlefield, 2004).

Page 160   The individual culture: Werner Jaeger, *Paideia: The Ideals of Greek Culture*, trans. Gilbert Highet (New York: Oxford University Press, 1965).

Page 161   For the early church: H. I. Marrou, *A History of Education in Antiquity*, trans. George Lamb (New York: Mentor, 1956), pp. 419-51.

Page 161   Christian schools as such: Ibid., p. 434.

Page 162   The guiding light: See the helpful summary of Old Testament spirituality in Deryck Sheriffs, *The Friendship of the Lord* (Carlisle: Paternoster, 1996).

Page 163   Scholars disagree: J. Jeremias, *The Prayers of Jesus* (London: SCM, 1967).

Page 164   Even the cantatas of Bach: Yaakov Elman and Israel Gershom, *Translating Jewish Traditions: Orality, Textuality and Cultural Diffusion* (New Haven, Conn.: Yale University Press, 2000), p. 252.

Page 164   "The task of the spiritual father": Kallistos Ware, "The Spiritual Father in Orthodox Christianity," *Cross Currents* 24 (1997): 308-9.

Page 169   "Just as I have a memory": Augustine *Confessions* 10 20.

Page 169   "We cannot properly say": Quoted by Gary Wills, *Saint Augustine's Memory* (New York: Viking, 2002), p. 8.

Page 170   "Making present the voices": Mary J. Carruthers, *The Book of Memory: A Study of Memory in Medieval Culture* (Cambridge: Cambridge University Press, 1990), p. 260.

Page 170   "Of the subtlety": Ibid., p. 3.

Page 171   "The more by the bond": Quoted by Wills, *Saint Augustine's Memory*, p. 19.

Epilogue: Communal Maturity in Christ

Page 173   "Everyone now strives": Fyodor Dostoyevsky, *The Brothers Karamazov*, trans. Richard Pevear and Larissa Volokhonsky (New York: Vintage

                    1990), pp. 303-4.

Page 175   "[At school,] When you took the problem": C. S. Lewis, *Reflections on the Psalms* (London: Geoffrey Bles, 1958), pp. 1-2.

Page 176   As Ivan Illich: David Cayley, *The Rivers North of the Future: The Testament of Ivan Illich* (Toronto: House of Anansi, 2005), pp. x, 56, 59.

Page 177   There are three things: Richard L. Thulin, *The "I" of the Sermon: Autobiography in the Sermon* (Minneapolis: Fortress, 1989), pp. 66-69.

Page 178   Like Daniel: John R. Sommerfeldt, *On the Spirituality of Relationship* (New York: Newman, 2004), p. 13.

Page 178   "Here we are": Aelred of Rievaulx, *Spiritual Friendship*, trans. Mary Eugenia Laker (Kalamzoo, Mich.: Cistercian, 1977), p. 51.

Page 178   "You can't write": Quoted in Cayley, *The Rivers North*, p. 152.

Page 179   It became fashionable: Peter Ramus, *Arguments in Rhetoric Against Quintillian*, trans. Carole Newlands (DeKalb: Northern Illinois University Press, 1986), p. 99.

Page 180   "By means of him": Calvin *Institutes* 1.13.14.

Page 180   "The proper condition": Calvin *Commentary on Ephesians* 1.10.

Page 180   Calvin interpreted the nature: Daphne Hampson, *Christian Contradictions* (London: Cambridge University Press, 2001), p. 35.

Page 180   Nature was a relational: John Calvin, *Instruction in Faith*, trans. Paul T. Fuhrmann (Louisville, Ky.: Westminster John Knox, 1992), p. 24.

Page 180   "What is the use": Quoted by John Bouwsma, *John Calvin: A Sixteenth Century Portait* (New York: Oxford University Press, 1988), p. 152.

Page 183   The least harmful interpretation: Charles Peguy, *Temporal and Eternal*, trans. Alexander Dru. (London: Harvill, 1958), p. 116.

Page 183   "When first thou didst entice": George Herbert, "Affliction."

Appendix: Why the Rhetoric of Dialectics?

Page 186   "None of you can pray": Martin Luther, quoted by Roland E. Murphy in *The Gift of the Psalms* (Peabody, Mass.: Hendrikson, 2003), p. ix.

Page 189   That is why Kierkegaard: Sylvia Walsh Utterback, "Kierkegaard's Inverse Dialectic," *Kierkegaardiana* XI (Copenhagen: C. A. Reitzel, 1980), pp. 34-54.

Page 189   "dying away to immediacy": Niels Thulstrup and Marie Mikulova Thulstrup, *The Sources and Depths of Faith in Kierkegaard,* Bibliotheca Kierkegaardiana (Copenhagen: C. A. Reitzels Boghandel, 1978), 2:163.

Index